TO NAV

Intelligent Learning
Competing in Systemic Chaos

All I am today, I owe to my mother,
I miss her unconditional love every second.

Ziad Makhzoumi

TABLE OF CONTENTS

"*If you wish to strive for peace of soul and happiness, then believe; if you wish to be a disciple of truth, then inquire.*"
–Friedrich Nietzsche

FOREWORD

Ziad Makhzoumi embodies *Intelligent Learning* by how he has successfully entered into a multitude of industry sectors to positively influence business with forward-thinking ideas. His trademark and signature strength is just this, to take learnings from one industry and finding new ways to apply them to others.

I first met Ziad in 2010. At that time he was already a long-established fixture on the UAE business scene. Ziad and I would come to work together in the summer of 2017 in the restructuring of a corporation that involved major changes on every level of the organisation. This is when Ziad shared his ideas on the book he was working on about his philosophy of Intelligent Learning. He invited me to join the project that has resulted in the book that you are now holding.

Observing Ziad in action, I have concluded that 'intelligence' and 'learning' are concepts that are often both misunderstood and underutilized. Intelligence, with the value and function it serves, is mainly dependent on our ability to learn. And how well we learn is about how intelligently we absorb and process information.

Whatever we set our sights on, whether we succeed or fail, it is most often a matter of having prepared more or less than our competitors. Compare it to a marathon; the race is not so much about the willpower displayed on the day, as much as it highlights the preparations made in the preceding months. And running a marathon is simple; you put one foot in front of the other. However, '*simple*' does not necessarily mean '*easy*.' It is the same with learning. There is rarely any single part of the information we need that is particularly difficult to comprehend. Instead, it is everything put together that needs to be approached systematically, one step at a time, with consistency and perseverance.

Learning is not about a matter of any single problem met with a single solution. Obtaining results in learning is about incremental growth, every day. Just as with a marathon, the challenge of learning has nothing to do with taking big leaps forward in short bursts. Intelligent Learning is about raising our game to the highest level, and having the stamina to sustain that and never stop evolving.

Central to the ideas in this book is the need for Intelligent Learning to be able to adapt to Systemic Chaos, the term Ziad Makhzoumi uses to describe the new normal in the modern business environment. What he refers to is the reality we are in where technological and political change is on the verge of perpetually upending almost every sector. In this setting, not responding quickly enough makes it inevitable that you perish and decay as faster and more nimble competitors take over.

Competing in a business environment of Systemic Chaos means having faster access to information and the ability to interpret it better to make predictions. This is what will give you the edge you need to place bets on what will work and what won't. Sometimes you are right, only not soon enough. Other times it turns out that what is real doesn't matter, or that what matters is not real. A large part of this game is gauging the perception of risk. In other words, interpreting what everyone around us is thinking.

Where Western tradition of thinking critically and independently has historically lent itself well to scientific and technological innovation, the question is now, with the increasing expectations on social conformity, are still living in the same environment thriving to seek new knowledge and technological advancement? Intelligent Learning goes back to the basics and approaches learning in a scientific way. It is a cognitive approach to better perceive and analyze information for sound decision-making. The method Ziad Makhzoumi presents in this book helps you navigate a path that circumvents the mental blocks that impede our judgment, both as individuals and as a group.

Despite the world now having better access to information and becoming more scientifically minded, collectively we are less able to question simple facts openly. Most agree that the social and political climate in the West has become more and more tribal, where facts are less important and winning arguments is more about expressing emotion. We seem to unconsciously gravitate towards the prevailing vision of the group to which we belong, and seal ourselves off collectively from absorbing any feedback that deviates from our consensual reality. In this bubble mentality, arguments are not based on the underlying facts. Instead, any conclusions drawn are predetermined, without any empirical evidence taken into consideration.

Our primary assumptions about a situation, and the initial decisions we base our plan on, without any allowance for course correction along the way, can turn out to be completely false and fundamentally unfounded. One can see this in how many problems are approached almost religiously and disagreeing on facts is done as a matter of proving your devotion to a faith. Under such circumstances, finding real answers to problems is almost impossible.

We are all prone to defend our beliefs with cherry-picked facts. Breaking through this bubble is a must to move beyond thinking that is motivated by self-interest for our reputation and our tribe. Our motivations for everything we do are social to some extent. We're always concerned to look good in the eyes of others. We're always concerned to help our team win and to make it clear that we're on our team's side, as well as being against the other side. This is an obstacle to Intelligent Learning: we are not programmed to seek the truth. Even though we may believe otherwise, seeking the truth is not our aim when we observe and reason. Furthermore, the greater the complexity and the higher the IQ of the people involved, the more stronger this 'willful blindness' appears to be. This is not due to any deliberately sinister motives. Simply, being more intelligent does not automatically make a person better at perceiving, interpreting and learning. A higher IQ will make you better at reasoning but also better at finding reasons to support your bias. It is easy to see how we are not programmed at finding arguments that support the opposing side.

Take even the sharpest group of people on the same side of an argument and the same interests, they are unlikely to find the answers with an accurate understanding truth a particular issue that matters to them. Intelligent Learning teaches an approach to counter being impeded from crucially testing opposing theories by seeking corroborating evidence and systematically challenging these. Without this approach, flawed thinking presents a fatal danger to any organisation.

Intelligent Learning can be applied in every walk of life, whether it is in business or learning to grow and expand your understanding of the world. To address weaknesses and blind spots, we first have to know what these are. Honestly acknowledging our weaknesses is probably the most difficult lessons to learn and take to heart. It is even more difficult than actually doing what is needed to take corrective action.

The text ahead can be seen as a call to accept this challenge. Very rarely can success be explained as having been a matter of luck. No matter where you are from, or what your circumstances are, how well you perform, and the results you achieve will mostly be about the preparations you have made and the work you put in to first learn and put in practice.

Oscar Wendel
Stockholm, 2018

"He who learns but does not think, is lost!
He who thinks but does not learn is in great danger"
–Confucius

INTRODUCTION

I am not claiming full ownership of the intellectual input in this book which I call an integrated approach to knowledge.

I am a collector of know-how and an integrator of experiences of what works in business, my approach creates more value for it puts together the same components differently but create value that will grow exponentially instead of sequentially.

Most of my career I have been frustrated with people who are not interested in learning new things and making things better, they chose not to be aware of what is around them and are content with looking in one direction instead of seeing everything that is really there. They hear but never listen. They look but do not observe.

We need to all be game changers, innovators, playing the game of business differently, we must have a new strategy for playing the same game with the rules that are now are out of date and for sure out of synch.

The world is changing faster than ever, its resources are not utilized efficiently, its economic systems are not working, and instead of learning new ways we bury our heads in the sand and do not see or hear and learn but wish for something different to happen instead of making it happen.

The game is still the same for the players in the business league, driven by short-term views, frustration and fear. The world is at war with itself fueled by ideologies and economic and cultural assumptions that do not work together anymore, old assumptions that are unreal that assume away risk by assuming the same risks that we know and not the new mutated risks that need different treatments. The world is going into a state of systematic chaotic disorganization, and unless we do something soon, that starts by learning the cause and the reasons we can never make it livable.

We must learn differently.

It is interesting to highlight the fact that the empirical data supporting the proposition that intelligence tests are not necessary for the definition of a learning disability.

Four assumptions of the use of IQ test scores in the definition of learning disabilities were examined. These assumptions were (a) IQ tests measure intelligence; (b) intelligence and achievement are independent, and the presence of a learning disability will not affect IQ scores; (c) IQ scores predict reading, and children with low IQ scores should be poor readers; and (d) reading disabled children with different IQ scores have different cognitive processes and information skills.

It was argued that IQ scores measure factual knowledge, expressive language abilities, and short-term memory, among other skills, and that because children with learning disabilities have deficits in these areas, their scores may be spuriously low. It also showed that some children with low IQ scores could be good readers, indicating that low IQ scores do not necessarily result in poor reading skills.

Empirical evidence showed that poor readers at a variety of IQ levels show similar reading, spelling, language, and memory deficits. On logical and empirical grounds, IQ test scores are not necessary for the definition of learning disabilities.

The human mind can learn fast but also has the tendency to define things or experiences as the opposite of something else. It prefers to define events as measurable outcomes, as something that is there or is not.

One dictionary has the following definition of Learning that we believe is relevant:

Learning: the activity or process of gaining knowledge or skill by studying, practicing, being taught, or experiencing something: the activity of someone who learns or knowledge or skill gained from learning.

The same dictionary defines the opposite of learning as: Ignore / lose / miss / misunderstand / overlook / teach

We need to learn differently and learn how to teach ourselves and learn quickly and smartly. There is something wrong with the learning process when teaching is considered as the opposite of learning; even teachers have to learn to teach differently.

I would like to thank Professor Tony Buzan for his valuable views on Intelligent Learning that energized the many open discussions we had over drinks and cigars. He is a dear friend and a very Intelligent Learner.

Ziad Makhzoumi
Dubai, 2018

CHAPTER 1

Definitions:

Reality:

The state of things as they actually exist, as opposed to an idealistic or notional idea of them. The state or quality of having existence or substance

New:

Produced, introduced, or discovered recently or now for the first time; not existing before. Already existing but seen, experienced, or acquired recently or now for the first time.

THE NEW REALITIES

The Industrial Revolution of the late 18th and early 19th centuries changed every aspect of our lives. Today our world is undergoing an even more dramatic transition due to new forces that are changing our global economy and our world as we know it.

Compared with the Industrial Revolution, this change is happening many times faster with a more significant impact. Although we all know that these forces are happening, most of us fail to comprehend their full magnitude and effects that will result. They are like waves; each wave can amplify one another, as they interact with, coincide with, and feed upon one another.

Corporations are a combination of assets, processes managed by people that have to survive and grow like any human in a permanently changing world. Today our world is undergoing an even more dramatic transition than during the Industrial Revolution due to the combined and exponential influence of these forces.

Compared with the Industrial Revolution, this change is happening ten times faster and at 300 times the scale with 3,000 times the impact.

Fast Technological Change: Technology has always been a great force in overturning the status quo. The difference today is the sheer influence of technology in our lives and the speed of change. Facebook attracted 6 million users in its first year, and that number multiplied 100 times over the next five years. China's mobile text- and voice-messaging service WeChat has 300 million users, more than the entire adult population of the United

LEARN INTELLIGENTLY OR DIE - FUTURE SHOCK

Future Shock is the title of a book written by Alvin Toffler in 1970, with the premise that too rapid technological change could have a profound psychological effect on both people and whole societies. He contended that the world was moving from an "industrial" to a "super-industrial" society and that the accelerated rate of change left people disoriented and disconnected from society – a paralysis caused by information overload. Toffler wrote this before the invention of the personal computer and the mobile telephone, and thirty years before the communications revolution brought about by the Internet. Recent developments can have only exacerbated the shattering stress and disorientation identified in his book and those not learning to adapt may well be victims of evolution in action.

States. Whereas it took more than 50 years after the telephone was invented until half of the American homes had one and it took 38 years for the radio to attract 50 million listeners.

Accelerated adoption invites accelerated innovation. At the end of the last decade, and two years after the iPhone's launch, developers had created around 150,000 applications, but that number had hit 1.2 million in 2014, and users had downloaded more than 75 billion total apps, more than ten for every person on the planet. Innovation has multiplied and spread in recent years but is poised to change and grow at an exponential speed beyond the power of human intuition to anticipate.

Processing power and connectivity are only part of the story. Their impact is multiplied by the data revolution, which places unprecedented amounts of information in the hands of consumers and businesses alike, and the proliferation of technology-enabled business models, from online retail platforms to car-hailing apps to cars that drive themselves and park themselves. The impact on our daily lives will be that more and more people will enjoy a new age of instant communication and limitless information that could facilitate and amplify knowledge, as well as confuse and disconnect people.

Urbanization: Urbanization is the shifting economic activity and dynamism to emerging markets and cities within those markets. These emerging markets are going through simultaneous technological and urban revolutions, shifting the center of the world economy east and south at a speed never before witnessed. By 2025, when China is projected to be home to more large companies than either the United States or Europe, it is expected that nearly half of the world's large companies to be headquartered in emerging markets because growth has moved elsewhere. Nearly half of global GDP growth between 2010 and 2025 will come from 440 cities in emerging markets—95 percent of them small- and medium-size cities not heard of before.

Technology allows businesses to start and gain scale with stunning speed while using little capital. Entrepreneurs and start-ups now frequently enjoy advantages over large, established business- es. The fast pace of technological innovation is shortening the life cycle of companies and forcing stakeholders to make decisions and commit resources much more quickly.

Aging Population: In the First World the population is getting older while in many Arab and African countries there is a de- mographic bubble of underemployed people under the age of 25. Fertility is falling, and the world's population is graying dramat- ically. While aging has been evident in developed economies for some time—Japan and Russia have seen their populations decline over the past few years. While the trend in appears to have been reversed in Russia —the demographic deficit is now spreading to China and soon will reach Latin America. Japan has recorded virtually zero economic growth for the last decade, but this may soon get seen as admirable performance considering the changes to its demographics and labor market.

For the first time in human history, aging could mean that the planet's population will plateau in most of the world. By 2013, about 60 percent of the world's population lived in countries with fertility rates below the replacement rate.

The European Commission expects that by 2060, Germany's population will shrink by one-fifth, and the number of people of working age will fall from 54 million in 2010 to 36 million in 2060. China's labor force peaked in 2012, and there is a fear that China will get old before it gets rich. In Thailand, the fertility rate has fallen from 5 in the 1970s to 1.4 today. A smaller workforce will place a greater onus on productivity for driving growth and may cause us to rethink the economy's potential and caring for large numbers of retired people will put severe pressure on government finances.

Greater Global Connections: The final force is the degree to which the world is much more connected through trade and movements in capital, people, and information. Trade and finance have long been part of the globalization story but, in recent decades, there has been another significant shift.

Instead of a series of lines connecting major trading hubs in Europe and North America, the global trading system has expanded into a complex web. Asia is becoming the world's largest trading region. Global capital flows expanded 25 times between 1980 and 2007. More than one billion people crossed borders in 2009, over five times the number in 1980, a phenomenon which has not been without political consequences in those populations who feel themselves the victims of globalization.

Learning to Learn Differently: These forces gathered pace, grew in scale, and started collectively to have a material impact on the world economy around the turn of the 21st century causing disrupting long-established patterns in virtually every market and every sector of the world economy and in every aspect of our lives. They are causing trends to simply break and force our world to change radically from the one in which many of us grew up, prospered, and formed learning skills that are so vital to our decision-making. Many of the assumptions, tendencies, and habits that had long proved so reliable have suddenly lost much of their relevance. We have never had more data and advice at our fingertips, yet we work in a world where professional forecasters routinely get caught unaware of information they should have been monitoring. That is partly because our historic learning still underpins much of our decision-making. Our intuition was largely formed by our experiences and ideas about how things worked during a time when changes were somewhat predictable.

In the new world, we all need to scrutinize our learnings and ways of learning and reset them if necessary. There is a great deal of work to be done. We need to realize that much of what we think we know about how the world works are wrong or do not apply anymore; we need to identify the long-standing trends that are breaking or do not apply to our new world, and to develop the courage and foresight to clear the intellectual arrogance and pretense. These lessons apply equally to governments, policymakers, educators and business leaders, and makes up a process to reset our internal navigation systems for the new unchartered journey that needs to be done now.

As humans, with all our ingenuity, inventiveness, and imagination, we tend to be slow to adapt to change. We seek false comfort by wanting the future to look much like the recent past. Reassessing our assumptions about the world and gaining a clearer perspective on how to negotiate the changing landscape will help us prepare to survive. We have to change how we look at things and see the obvious that we took for granted. And the classic approach to strategy that assumes that with sufficient generated analytical and adequate assessment of the probabilities; strategists can pave a predictable path to the future from the learnings of the past. This approach does not work anymore for it "assumes away" most risk.

We need different approaches that no longer rely on the belief that the future is foreseeable and that defining and achieving an enduring competitive advantage is just an arrogant conceit that needs to stop, a delusion to be treated and a corporate illness to be cured.

Although the pace of change continues to accelerate, the fundamental transformations underway in the global economy are not yet complete. Like any other processes that influence our lives, if we start early, we can learn faster and manage the change better. Only 20 percent of the world's GDP comes from industries that can be called global, and it will take 30 years or more before anything reasonably approaching a genuinely integrated global economy can be realized. The result is an economic environment marked by a substantial increase in awareness of new risk and aversion to it.

Corporations Must Learn to Learn Differently:
Corporate strategy today has to align itself to the fluid, unpredictable nature of this new external environment. It must be flexible enough to constantly adapt to the outside and internal conditions. Corporations must learn about the new world differently and with constant re-invention.

LEARN INTELLIGENTLY OR DIE: KODAK

For most of the 20th Century, Kodak held a dominant global position in the manufacture of photographic film (with one of the world's most recognizable brand logos), but its key executives did not see or did not appreciate the speed at which digital photography would make film obsolete. From a peak of nearly $16bn in revenues in 1997, Kodak filed for bankruptcy in 2012 and sold a portfolio of its patents to the new leaders of the technology world (including Apple, Google, Facebook, and Amazon) for $525m. It emerged from bankruptcy as a much smaller digital printing and services business.

Learning Differently Breeds Opportunity: Corporate strategy is evolving and becoming increasingly about gaining competitive advantage through new knowledge and learning differently. In today's increasingly global fluid economic environment, confusion about risk is like the obstacles in a race track. Familiarity makes them less dangerous. As the global economy evolves, and as geographic markets and industry structures aggregate, participants will enjoy a variety of advantages from being aware and a variety of disadvantages from not doing so.

Companies choosing to compete only where they have significant advantages of familiarity make it highly probable that they can prosper even amid a high level of complexity and uncertainty. This is where learning fast and differently, will help. Much of the needed knowledge can come only through experimentation, by learning from those experiences which should include testing the new value proposition.

There must be a willingness to change direction continually as more and more specialised knowledge is acquired. Certain companies already use this approach in at least some of their strategic decision-making processes. The pharmaceutical industry has long used such disciplined processes to develop new drugs and medical devices, and so have venture capital firms, with their portfolios of companies.

Three distinct elements are central to this approach, all driven by the new learning process. First, it entails a disciplined search, based on systematic learning, to discover and create initiatives that provide disproportionately high rewards for the risks taken. Second, it involves a dynamic, continuous effort to manage the portfolio of initiatives to overcome inescapable risks due to

Ziad Makhzoumi

Learning Differently Breeds Opportunity: Corporate strategy is evolving and becoming increasingly about gaining competitive advantage through new knowledge and learning differently. In today's increasingly global fluid economic environment, confusion about risk is like the obstacles in a race track. Familiarity makes them less dangerous. As the global economy evolves, and as geographic markets and industry structures aggregate, participants will enjoy a variety of advantages from being aware and a variety of disadvantages from not doing so.

Companies choosing to compete only where they have significant advantages of familiarity make it highly probable that they can prosper even amid a high level of complexity and uncertainty. This is where learning fast and differently, will help. Much of the needed knowledge can come only through experimentation, by learning from those experiences which should include testing the new value proposition.

There must be a willingness to change direction continually as more and more specialised knowledge is acquired. Certain companies already use this approach in at least some of their strategic decision-making processes. The pharmaceutical industry has long used such disciplined processes to develop new drugs and medical devices, and so have venture capital firms, with their portfolios of companies.

Three distinct elements are central to this approach, all driven by the new learning process. First, it entails a disciplined search, based on systematic learning, to discover and create initiatives that provide disproportionately high rewards for the risks taken. Second, it involves a dynamic, continuous effort to manage the portfolio of initiatives to overcome inescapable risks due to

LEARN INTELLIGENTLY OR DIE: IBM

Known as "Big Blue", International Business Machines started out its life as a manufacturer of mechanical adding machines but became famous for its wholesale dominance of the mainframe computer market in the 1970s and 1980s. It also invented the Personal Computer ("PC") but was unable to predict that Moore's Law that posits that computer chips double in speed and halve in price every eighteen months. This would eventually allow the PC to make mainframes obsolete in all but the most specialised of applications. IBM could easily have gone the way of Kodak but in 1993 hired for the first time an outsider, Louis Gerstner, who used the legacy cash flow and financial strength to transform it into a software and services business.

complexity and uncertainty by learning dynamically. Finally, it calls for a flexible and evolutionary approach that lets "natural selection" guide the vision and not only personal beliefs and egos.

A company must organize a disciplined search to identify, enhance, and nurture its best ideas—and deploy some of its most talented people to pursue them—if it wants to create real opportunities to earn high returns relative to the risks taken. Checkpoint reviews, milestones, and staged actions enable managers to make maximum progress while minimizing risk. Risks arising from complexity and uncertainty fade as time passes, due to the range of outcomes reduced, all with the intent of learning better.

A successful corporate strategy involves creating enough initiatives offering high returns relative to the risks taken to enable a company to meet its aspirations and meet the expectations of the capital markets, while increasingly taking account of non-financial requirements such as corporate and social responsibility and wider stakeholder interests imposed by political constraints.

Inherent in this approach is the understanding that future decisions and future outcomes are likely to vary enormously from initial hypotheses. The whole process combines an approach that combines art and science. Most of the critical decisions involve subjective judgments that, unlike those generated by more deterministic strategies, will be formed by knowledge gained as time passes and by iterative techniques.

Although the world is increasingly complex, confusing, and uncertain, serendipity does not have to be more important than skill in the crafting and implementing of corporate strategy.

As the global environment continually changes and risk levels rise, a portfolio-of-initiatives approach holds out the opportunity for corporations to be as flexible and adaptive as the markets themselves.

THE LAST MAN TO KNOW EVERYTHING

Many men have been accorded the title of "The Last Man to Know Everything", i.e., able to know the whole body of scientific and philosophical learning extant in the world at the time they lived. Sometime after 1700, it began to be obvious that no one person could possibly absorb all the increasing body of scientific knowledge, but at the two ends of the scale are probably Aristotle (d322 BC) and Johann Goethe (d1823).

CHAPTER 2

Learn Intelligently

One definition of learning is the alteration of behavior as a result of individual experience. When an organism can perceive and change its behavior, it is said to learn.

On the subject of learning, Plato (428-347 B.C.) proposed the question: How does an individual learn something new when the topic is brand new to that person?

This question may seem trivial; however, think of a human as a computer. The question would then become: How does a computer take in any factual information without having been previously programmed?

Plato answered his question by stating that knowledge is present at birth and all information learned by a person is merely a recollection of something the soul has already learned previously, which is called the Theory of Recollection or Platonic epistemology. This answer could be further justified by the paradox: 'if a person knows something, then they will not need to question it, and if a person does not know something, then they will not know to question it at all.'

Plato says that if one did not previously know something, then they cannot learn it. He describes learning as a passive process of ironing information and knowledge into the soul over time. However, Plato's theory elicits even more questions about knowledge: If we can only learn something when we already had the knowledge impressed onto our souls, then how did our souls gain that knowledge in the first place? Plato's theory can seem convoluted; however, his classical theory can help us understand knowledge until this day.

John Locke (1632-1704) offered an answer to Plato's question as well. John Locke offered the "blank slate" theory where humans are born into the world with no innate knowledge. He recognized that something had to be present, however. This something, to John Locke, seemed to be "mental powers." Locke viewed these powers as a natural ability the baby is born with, similar to how a baby automatically knows how to function in a biological sense when it is born. So as soon as the baby enters the world, it immediately has experiences with its surroundings, and all of those experiences get transcribed to the baby's "slate." All of the experiences then eventually culminate in complex and abstract ideas. This theory can still help teachers understand their humans' learning today.

Irrespective of which approach we use for learning, what is important is to understand the process and to map it accurately. This is to improve on it or selectively direct it for the objective is the outcome, that is, what we can measure and define as a success or a failure.

LEARNING BEHAVIORS

A wide array of learned behaviors have been mapped and include: Discrimination Learning: a subject learns to respond to a limited range of sensory characteristics, such as a particular shade of coloration; Habituation: the cessation of responses to repeated stimulation, Concept Formation: the process of sorting experiences according to related features; Problem Solving and Perceptual Learning: the effects of past experience on sensory perceptions, and Psychomotor Learning: the development of neuromuscular patterns in response to sensory signals. To understand how we learn we must enter the world of behavior analysis or behaviorism.

John Watson (1878–1959) introduced the term "behaviorism," he believed the behaviorist view is a purely objective experimental branch of natural science with a goal to predict and control behavior. In an article in the Psychological Review, he stated that "its theoretical goal is the prediction and control of behavior. Introspection forms no essential part of its methods, nor is the scientific value of its data dependent upon the readiness with which they lend themselves to interpretation concerning consciousness." Behaviorism has since become one of three domains of behavior analysis, the other two being the Experimental Analysis of Behavior, and Applied Behavior Analysis.

Methodological behaviorism is based on the theory of treating public events, or observable behavior. B.F. Skinner introduced another type of behaviorism called radical behaviorism, or the Conceptual Analysis of Behavior, which is based on the theory of treating private events; for example, thinking and feeling. Radical behaviorism forms the conceptual piece of behavior analysis.

In behavior analysis, learning is the acquisition of a new behavior through conditioning and social learning. There are three types of conditioning and learning:

• Classical conditioning: behavior becomes a reflex response to an antecedent stimulus.

• Operant conditioning: Consequence of a behavior follows antecedent stimuli through a reward (reinforcement) or a punishment.

• Social learning theory: Observation of behavior is followed by modeling.

Ivan Pavlov discovered classical conditioning. He observed that if dogs come to associate the delivery of food with a white lab coat or with the ringing of a bell, they will produce saliva, even when there is no sight or smell of food. Classical conditioning regards this form of learning to be the same whether in dogs or humans. Operant conditioning reinforces this behavior with a reward or a punishment. A reward increases the likelihood of the behavior recurring; a punishment decreases its likelihood. Social learning theory observes behavior and is followed with modeling.

These three learning theories form the basis of applied behavior analysis, the application of behavior analysis, which uses analyzed antecedents, functional analysis, replacement behavior strategies, and often data collection and reinforcement to change behavior. The old practice was called behavior modification, which only used assumed antecedents and consequences to change behavior without acknowledging the conceptual analysis; analyzing the function of behavior and teaching new behaviors that would serve the same function was never relevant in behavior modification.

Behaviorists view the learning process as a change in behavior and will arrange the environment to elicit desired responses through such devices as behavioral objectives, Competency-based learning, and skill development and training. Educational approaches such as Early Intensive Behavioral Intervention, curriculum-based measurement, and direct instruction have emerged from this model.

TRANSFER OF LEARNING

Transfer of Learning is the idea that what one learns in school somehow carries over to situations different from that particular time and that particular setting. Transfer of Learning was among the first phenomena tested in educational psychology. Edward Lee Thorndike was a pioneer in transfer research. He found that though Transfer of Learning is extremely important for learning and that it is a rarely occurring phenomenon. Thorndike held an experiment where he had the subjects estimate the size of a specific shape and then he would switch the shape. He found that the prior information did not help the subjects; instead, it impeded their learning.

One explanation of why Transfer of Learning does not occur often can be explained in terms of surface structure and deep structure. The surface structure is the way a problem is framed. The deep structure is the set of steps for the solution. For example, when a math story problem changes contexts from asking how much it costs to reseed a lawn to how much it costs to varnish a table, they have different surface structures, but the steps for getting the answers are the same. Many people are more influenced by the surface structure. In reality, the surface structure is unimportant. Nonetheless, people are concerned with it because they believe that it will give them background knowledge on how to do the problem. Consequently, this interferes with people's understanding of the deep structure of the problem. Even if somebody is trying to concentrate on the deep structure, transfer of learning may still be unsuccessful because the deep structure is not usually very obvious. Therefore, surface structure gets in the way of people's ability to see the deep structure of the problem and transfer the knowledge they have learned to come up with a solution to a new problem.

Richard Bandler and John Grinder studied this process which the basis of, Neuro-Linguistic Programming ("NLP") and applied in techniques for changing behavior.

Current learning pedagogies focus on conveying rote knowledge, independent of the context within which gives it meaning. Because of this, humans often struggle to transfer this stand-alone information into other aspects of their education. Humans need much more than abstract concepts and self-contained knowledge; they need exposure to learning practiced in the context of authentic activity and culture.

Critics of situated cognition, however, would argue that by discrediting stand-alone information, the transfer of knowledge across contextual boundaries becomes impossible. There must be a balance between situating knowledge while also grasping the deep structure of the material or the understanding of how one arrives to know such information.

Some theorists argue that transfer does not even occur at all. They believe that humans transform what they have learned into the new context. They say that transfer is too much of a passive notion. They believe humans, instead, transform their knowledge in an active way. Humans don't simply carry over knowledge from the classroom; they construct the knowledge in a way that they can understand themselves. The learner changes the information they have learned to make it best adapt to the changing contexts that they use the knowledge in. This transformation process can occur when a learner feels motivated to use the knowledge; however, if the person does not find the transformation necessary, it is less likely that the knowledge will transform.

TECHNIQUES AND BENEFITS

Many different conditions influence Transfer of Learning in the classroom. These conditions include features of the task, features of the learner, features of the organization and social context of the activity. The features of the task include practicing through simulations, problem-based learning, and knowledge and skills for implementing new plans. The features of learners include their ability to reflect on past experiences, their ability to participate in group discussions, practice skills, and participate in written discussions. All of the unique features will contribute to a student's ability to use Transfer of Learning. There are structural techniques that can aid learning transfer in the classroom. These structural strategies include hugging and bridging.

Hugging uses the technique of simulating an activity to encourage reflexive learning. An example of the hugging strategy is when a student practices teaching a lesson or when a student role plays with another student. These examples encourage critical thinking which will engage the student and help them understand what they are learning which is one of the goals of transfer of learning.

Bridging is when instruction encourages thinking abstractly by helping to identify connections between ideas and to analyze those connections. An example is when a teacher lets the student analyze their past test results and the way in which they got those results. This includes the amount of study time and study strategies. By looking at their past study strategies, it can help them come up with strategies in the future to improve their performance. These are some of the ideas that are important to successful practices of hugging and bridging. There are many benefits of transfer of learning in the classroom. One of the main benefits is the ability to learn a new task quickly. This has many real-life applications such as language and speech processing. Transfer of learning is also very useful in teaching humans to use higher cognitive thinking by applying their background knowledge to new situations.

COGNITIVISM

Cognitive theories grew out of Gestalt psychology. Wolfgang Kohler developed Gestalt psychology in Germany in the early 1900s and came to America in the 1920s. The German word gestalt is roughly equivalent to the English configuration or organization and emphasizes the whole of human experience. Over the years, the Gestalt psychologists provided demonstrations and described principles to explain the way we organize our sensations into perceptions. Matt Wertheimer, one of the founding fathers of Gestalt Theory, observed that sometimes we interpret motion when there is no motion at all. For example, a powered sign used at a convenience store to indicate that the store is open or closed might be seen as a sign with "flashing lights." However, the lights are not actually flashing. The lights have been programmed to blink rapidly at their own individual pace. Perceived as a whole, the sign flashes. Perceived individually, the lights turn off and on at designated times. Another example of this would be a brick house: As a whole, it is viewed as a standing structure. However, it is actually composed of many smaller parts, which are individual bricks. People tend to see things from a holistic point of view rather than breaking it down into sub-units.

In Gestalt theory, psychologists say that instead of obtaining knowledge from what's in front of us, we often learn by making sense of the relationship between what's new and old. Because we have a unique perspective of the world, humans can generate their own learning experiences and interpret information that may or may not be the same for someone else.
Gestalt psychologists criticize behaviorists for being too dependent on overt behavior to explain learning. They propose looking

at the patterns rather than isolated events. Gestalt views of learning have been incorporated into what have come to be labeled cognitive theories. Two key assumptions underlie this cognitive approach: that the memory system is an active, organized processor of information and that prior knowledge plays an important role in learning. Gestalt theorists believe that for learning to occur prior knowledge must exist on the topic. When the learner applies their prior knowledge to the advanced topic, the learner can understand the meaning in the advanced topic and learning can occur. Cognitive theories that look beyond behavior and considers how human memory works to promote learning, gives an understanding of short-term memory and long-term memory is important to educators influenced by cognitive theory. They view learning as an internal mental process (including insight, information processing, memory and perception) where the educator focuses on building intelligence and cognitive development. The individual learner is more important than the environment.

OTHER COGNITIVE THEORIES

The establishment of memory theories like the Atkinson-Shiffrin memory model and Baddeley's Working Memory Model, theoretical frameworks in cognitive psychology, gave way to new cognitive frameworks of learning that began to emerge during the 1970s, 80s, and 90s. Today, researchers concentrate on topics like cognitive load and information processing theory. These theories of learning play a role in influencing instructional design. Cognitive Theory is used to explain topics such as Social Role Acquisition, intelligence and, memory as related to age.

In the late twentieth century, situated cognition emerged as a theory that recognized current learning as primarily the transfer of decontextualized and formal knowledge. Bredo (1994) depicts situated cognition as "shifting the focus from individual in the environment to individual and environment." In other words, individual cognition should be considered as intimately related to the context of social interactions and culturally constructed meaning. Learning through this perspective, in which known and doing become inseparable, becomes both applicable and whole.

Much of the education humans receive is limited to the culture of schools and without consideration for authentic cultures outside of education. Curricula framed by situated cognition can bring knowledge to life by embedding the learned material within the culture that humans are familiar. For example, the formal and abstract syntax of math problems can be transformed by placing a traditional math problem within a practical story problem. This method presents an opportunity to meet that appropriate balance between situated and transferable knowledge.
Lampert (1987) successfully did this by having humans explore mathematical concepts that are continuous with their background knowledge. She did so by using money, something everyone is familiar with, and then developed the lesson to include more complex stories that allow for humans to see various solutions as well as create their own. In this way, knowledge becomes active, evolving as humans participate and negotiate their way through new situations.

CONSTRUCTIVISM

Founded by Jean Piaget, constructivism emphasizes the importance of the active involvement of learners in constructing knowledge for themselves. Humans are thought to use background knowledge and concepts to assist them in their acquisition of novel information. When such new information is approached, the learner faces a loss of equilibrium with their previous understanding which demands a change in cognitive structure. This change effectively combines previous and novel information to form an improved cognitive schema. Constructivism can be both subjectively and contextually based. Under the theory of radical constructivism, coined by Ernst von Glasersfeld, understanding relies on one's subjective interpretation of experience as opposed to objective "reality". Similarly, William Cobern's idea of contextual constructivism encompasses the effects of culture and society on experience.

Constructivism asks why humans do not learn deeply by listening to a teacher or reading from a textbook. To design effective teaching environments, it believes one needs a good understanding of what children already know when they come into the classroom. The curriculum is ideally designed in a way so that builds on the pupil's background knowledge and is allowed to develop with them. Begin with complex problems and teach basic skills while solving these problems.

The learning theories of John Dewey, Maria Montessori, and David A. Kolb serve as the foundation of the application of constructivist learning theory in the classroom. Constructivism has many varieties such as active learning, discovery learning, and knowledge building, but all versions promote a student's free exploration within a given framework or structure. The teacher acts as a facilitator who encourages humans to discover principles for themselves and to construct knowledge by working answering open-ended questions and solving real-world problems. To do this, a teacher should encourage curiosity and discussion among his/her humans as well as promote their autonomy. In scientific areas in the classroom, constructivist teachers provide raw data and physical materials for the humans to work with and analyze.

TRANSFORMATIVE LEARNING

Transformative learning theory seeks to explain how humans revise and reinterpret meaning. Transformative learning is the cognitive process of effecting change in a frame of reference. A frame of reference defines our view of the world. The emotions are often involved. Adults tend to reject any ideas that do not correspond to their particular values, associations, and concepts.

Our frames of reference are composed of two dimensions: habits of mind and points of view. Habits of mind, such as ethnocentrism, are harder to change than points of view. Habits of mind influence our point of view and the resulting thoughts or feelings associated with them, but points of view may change over time as a result of influences such as reflection, appropriation, and feedback. Transformative learning takes place by discussing with others the "reasons presented in support of competing interpretations, by critically examining evidence, arguments, and alternative points of view. When circumstances permit, transformative learners move toward a frame of reference that is more inclusive, discriminating, self-reflective, and integrative of experience.

EDUCATIONAL NEUROSCIENCE

American Universities such as Harvard, Johns Hopkins, and the University of Southern California began offering majors and degrees dedicated to educational neuroscience or neuro-education in the first decade of the twenty-first century. Such studies seek to link an understanding of brain processes with classroom instruction and experiences. Neuro-education seeks to analyze the biological changes that take place in the brain as new information is processed. It looks at what environmental, emotional and social situations are best for new information to be retained and stored in the brain via the linking of neurons, rather than allowing the dendrites to be reabsorbed and the information lost. The 1990s were designated "The Decade of the Brain," and advances took place in neuroscience at an especially rapid pace. The three dominant methods for measuring brain activities are event-related potential, functional magnetic resonance imaging and magnetoencephalography (MEG).

The integration and application to education of what we know about the brain were strengthened in 2000 when the American Federation of Teachers stated: "It is vital that we identify what science tells us about how people learn to improve the education curriculum. What is exciting about this new field in education is that modern brain imaging techniques now make it possible, in some sense, to watch the brain as it learns, and the question then arises: can the results of neuro-scientific studies of brains, as they are learning usefully, inform practice in this area? Although the field of neuroscience is young, new technologies and ways to observe learning are expected. This will show new paradigms of what humans need and how humans learn best and will further refine the scientific evidence. In particular, those with learning disabilities will be taught using strategies that are more informed.

FORMAL AND MENTAL DISCIPLINE

All individuals can develop mental discipline and the skill of mind-fulness; the two go hand in hand. Mental discipline is huge in shaping what people do, say, think and feel. It's critical in the processing of information and involves the ability to recognize and respond appropriately to new information or recently learnings. Mindfulness is important to the process of learning in many aspects. Being mindful means to be present with and engaged in whatever you are doing at a specific moment in time. Being mindful can aid in helping us to more critically think, feel and understand the new information we are in the process of absorbing. The formal discipline approach seeks to develop causation between the advancement of the mind by exercising it through exposure to abstract school subjects such as science, language, and mathematics. With the student's repetitive exposure to these particular subjects, some scholars feel that the acquisition of knowledge about science, language, and math is of "secondary importance."

Furthermore, they believe that the strengthening and further development of the mind that this curriculum provides holds far greater significance for the progressing learner in the long haul. D.C. Phillips and Jonas F. Soltis provide some skepticism to this notion. Their skepticism stems largely in part from feeling that the relationship between formal discipline and the overall advancement of the mind is not as strong as some would say. They illustrate their hesitance to accept this idea by offering up the perspective that it is foolish to blindly assume that people will be better off in life or at performing certain tasks because of taking particular, yet unrelated courses.

THEORY OF MULTIPLE INTELLIGENCES

Psychologist Howard Gardner proposed the existence of multiple intelligences, suggesting that humans possess different kinds of intelligence. It is a theory that has been fashionable in Continuous Professional Development (CPD) training courses for teachers. However, the theory of multiple intelligences is often cited as an example of pseudoscience because it lacks empirical evidence or falsifiability.

MULTIMEDIA LEARNING

Multimedia learning refers to the use of visual and auditory teaching materials that may include video, computer, and other information technology. Multimedia learning theory focuses on the principles that determine the effective use of multimedia in learning, with emphasis on using both the visual and auditory channels for information processing.

The auditory channel deals with information that is heard, and the visual channel processes information that is seen. The visual channel holds less information than the auditory channel. If both the visual and auditory channels are presented with information, more knowledge is retained. However, if too much information is delivered, it is inadequately processed, and long-term memory is not acquired. Multimedia learning seeks to give instructors the ability to stimulate both the visual and auditory channels of the learner, resulting in better progress.

EDUCATIONAL GAMES AND VIDEO GAMES IN EDUCATION

Many educators and researchers believe that information technology could bring innovation in traditional educational. Teachers and technologists are searching for new and innovative ways to design learner-centered learning environments effectively, trying to engage learners more in the learning process. Claims have been made that online games have the potential to teach, train and educate and they are effective means of learning skills and attitudes that are not so easy to learn by rote memorization.

There has been a lot of research done in identifying the learning effectiveness in game-based learning. Learner characteristics and cognitive learning outcomes have been identified as the key factors in research on the implementation of games in educational settings. In the process of learning a language through an online game, there is a strong relationship between the learner's prior knowledge of that language and their cognitive learning outcomes. For the people with prior knowledge of the language, the learning effectiveness of the games is much more than those with none or less knowledge of the language.

OTHER LEARNING THEORIES

Other learning theories have also been developed for more specific purposes. For example, andragogy is the art and science to help adults learn. Connectivism is a recent theory of networked learning which focuses on learning as making connections. The Learning as a Network (LaaN) theory builds upon connectivism, complexity theory, and double-loop learning. It starts from the learner and views learning as the continuous creation of a personal knowledge network (PKN).

LEARNING STYLES

Learning style theories propose that individuals learn in different ways, that there are distinct learning styles and that knowledge of a learner's preferred learning style will lead to faster and more satisfactory improvement. There are a large number of untested, informal, theories that educators argue will add some benefit to learning.

INFORMAL AND POST-MODERN THEORIES

These are theories that make use of cognitive restructuring, an informal curriculum which promotes the use of prior knowledge to help humans gain a broad understanding of concepts. New knowledge cannot be told to humans, it believes, but rather the humans' current knowledge must be challenged. In this way, humans will adjust their ideas to more closely resemble actual theories or concepts. By using this method humans gain the broad understanding they're taught and later are more willing to learn and keep the specifics of the concept or theory. This theory further aligns with the idea that teaching the concepts and the language of a subject should be split into multiple steps.

Other informal learning theories look at the sources of motivation for learning. Intrinsic motivation may create a more self-regulated learner, yet schools undermine intrinsic motivation. Critics argue that the average student learning in isolation performs significantly less well than those learning with collaboration and mediation. Humans learn through talk, discussion, and argumentation.

PHILOSOPHICAL ANTHROPOLOGY

Another theory that Theodora Polito developed is that, "every well-constructed theory of education [has] at [its] center a philosophical anthropology," which is "a philosophical reflection on some basic problems of mankind. Philosophical anthropology is an exploration of human nature and humanity. Aristotle, an early influence on the field, deemed human nature to be "rational animality," wherein humans are closely related to other animals but still set apart by their ability to form rational thought.

Philosophical anthropology expanded upon these ideas by clarifying that rationality is "determined by the biological and social conditions in which the lives of human beings are embedded." Fully developed learning theories address some of the "basic problems of mankind" by examining these biological and social conditions in order to understand and manipulate the rationality of humanity in the context of learning.

Philosophical anthropology is evident in behaviorism, which requires an understanding of humanity and human nature in order to assert that the similarities between humans and other animals are critical and influential to the process of learning. Situated cognition focuses on how humans interact with each other and their environments, which would be considered the "social conditions" explored within the field of philosophical anthropology. Transformative learning theories operate with the assumption that humans are rational creatures capable of examining and redefining perspectives, something that is heavily considered within philosophical anthropology.

An awareness and understanding of philosophical anthropology contribute to a greater comprehension and practice of any learning theory. In some cases, philosophy can be used to further explore and define uncertain terms within the field of education. Philosophy can also be

a vehicle to explore the purpose of education, which can greatly influence an educational theory.

Critics of learning theories that seek to displace traditional educational
practices claim that there is no need for such theories; that the attempt
to comprehend the process of learning through the construction of
theories creates problems and inhibits personal freedom.
Whatever works and results in a positive outcome should be considered as a learning tool.

INTELLIGENCE

The origin of intelligent comes from Latin early 16th century: from Latin intelligent- 'understanding', from the verb intelligere, variant of intellegere 'understand', from inter 'between' + legere 'choose.'

Dictionaries define intelligent as follows:

Intelligent [in-tel-i-juh nt] adjective

• Having good understanding or a high mental capacity; quick to comprehend, characterized by quickness of understanding, sound thought, or good judgment.

• Having the faculty of reasoning and understanding.

• Bright. Intelligent, intellectual describe distinctive mental capacity. Intelligent often suggests a natural quickness of understanding: an intelligent reader. Intellectual implies not only having a high degree of understanding, but also a capacity and taste for the higher forms of knowledge: intellectual interests.

• Astute, clever, alert, bright, apt, discerning, shrewd, smart

• Having or showing the ability to easily learn or understand things or to deal with new or difficult situations; having or showing a lot of intelligence

• Able to learn and understand things

• Having an ability to deal with problems or situations that resembles or suggests the ability of an intelligent person

On the other hand, the human mind also defines a process or a state by its opposite. The same dictionaries define the antonyms of intelligent as:

Dark, Dull, Foolish, Idiotic, Ignorant, Imbecile, Normal, Old, Stupid, Typical, Unaware, Uncreative, Uneducated, Unimaginative, Unintelligent, Uninventive, Unreasonable, Un-resourceful, Worn are only a few. An interesting way of defining an outcome based on expectations.

LEARN OR DIE: THE STORY OF WANG AND DELL COMPUTERS

Learn or Die: The Story of Wang and Dell Computers:
Wang Laboratories was a small firm, started by Dr. An Wang in 1951, that grew to play a significant role in the development of the U.S. computer industry of the 1980s
Chinese immigrant An Wang, a Harvard Ph.D. and computer pioneer, turned a Boston storefront operation into one of the legendary success stories in the computer industry. But by 1985 the glory years at Wang Laboratories had given way to a downward spiral of massive debt, layoffs, and late product deliveries. Wang's trajectory resembles a classic tragedy, rooted in a fatal flaw of its secretive, visionary leader--his obsessive desire for control and his placing of family interests ahead of those of shareholders. Wang's biggest mistake was making his son Fred director of R&D, then president. Dr. Wang fired his son in 1989, a year before his death from cancer.
Wang was on top of the computing world in the late 20th century before a couple of guys named Bill (Gates) and Steve (Jobs) and their engineering whiz-kid pals, such as Apple's Steve Wozniak, began to rock Wang's world.
Massachusetts-based Wang was a pioneer in mini-computing, which was a better mousetrap than mainframe computing. The rise of the mini-computer dominated the tech landscape until something called "client-server computing" emerged in the late 1980s. The client-server generation is another name for the "personal computer era" – a time when PCs were connected to central

server computers via a network. The upshot: Mini-computers were quickly supplanted by faster, cheaper client-server networks, making the likes of Wang relatively obsolete.

Most observers point to the initial public offering of Microsoft in 1985 as the beginning of the client-server era as the software maker's Windows operating system fueled the rise of personal computers. Windows was so dominatingly successful that the federal courts deemed it a monopoly. Michael Dell's personal computer outfit was a big beneficiary of the Windows ecosystem, along with Intel, whose computer chips were designed to power personal computers using Windows.

Dell was to client-server computing as Wang was to mini-computing. However, all good things must come to an end, and for technology behemoths, the end seems to come sooner rather than later. The shelf lives of hugely successful tech giants tend to run shorter than other industrial giants because the velocity of change in information technology simply is more intensified than, say, the soap or steel businesses.

Critics and pundits have wrongly accused Dell founder, Michael Dell, of not being an innovator; he was solely a brilliant marketer that built personal computers cheaply. Yes, he was all that. But he did innovate. Dell created one of the greatest manufacturing and distribution models in business history. His build-to-order personal computer operation, which bypassed wholesalers and retailers by delivering custom-built machines directly to consumers and companies, was a masterstroke.

But the advantages of Dell's business model largely were eroded by the commoditization of the PC industry and the emergence of the laptop computer. Competitors, such as Hewlett-Packard, Lenovo, and Acer, eventually caught up.

Seeing the writing on the wall, IBM unloaded its PC business to China's Lenovo in 2005. It retooled and expanded into a one-stop shop for corporate technology needs, diversifying into software, storage, networking and most important, services and consulting. IBM is the rare breed that has traversed the rocky shoals of 'mainframe to client-server', to what is now the cloud-computing era.

Dell made the transition to a full-service provider of technology to corporate customers later rather than sooner. It remains a manufacturer of computers, servers, and other gear but has expanded into consulting with its acquisition of Perot Systems. But it probably was too little, too late to compete with Google, Amazon.com and other cloud-computing stalwarts.

As for Wang, it hung around for years after the rise of personal computers but never really recovered, filing for bankruptcy before being acquired. A privately held Dell could fare better, but regardless of the buyout drama, its best days are certainly in the rear-view mirror.

CHAPTER 3

DESIGNING INTELLIGENT HUMAN CAPITAL

The Learning Process

Success in any field requires the ability to perform effectively, consistently and efficiently in a wide range of conditions. It is a combination of knowing where you want to go and being able to get there.

Learning to do so should be an activity that works across this spectrum, bringing clarification and focus on what we want, helping us to establish what it takes to get there. Whatever the context, learning is about unlocking a person's potential so that they maximize their performance. This should be applied equally to organizations.

The rate and speed of change is dictated by a person's or organizations' internal capacity for change that is restricted by the resources available internally and externally. This capacity to change is defined as the ability to detect and implement successfully the necessary steps, in other words **learning how to change.**

Success can be learned: It is important starting the learning process by putting your mind in a state that you have had many times before, a state where you learned even without thinking consciously; how much information you absorbed during this process. This ability that you had the moment you were born. How to feed yourself, how to walk, how to express yourself and how to determine what you want. It came to you intuitively. However, although the ability is there, you had to learn the skills associated with the process of walking. Although you learned how to walk, you had to learn the many skills of how not to lose balance and keep an eye on things in front of you, on your side or even behind you. It is like learning how to learn again!

It is this ability to learn skills, and how to integrate them into our daily life so that you do them without thinking, or unconsciously, that will make you excel and be different from others. Those skills from reading to playing the piano to using computers, languages, sports are all skills that you learned when you wanted to.

If our brains are computers, then our thoughts are our software programs. We could change our mental programs, just as we do when we change or upgrade the software, either by changing it completely or by giving it different instructions. But like a computer no matter how much we want or hope, it will not upgrade our software on its own. Neither will entering the same instructions over and over again. What we need to do is to give new instructions to the current programs where it is necessary. With a computer, the way to do this is laid out in the manual provided with the software. With human beings, it has been more of a challenge, since there are no manuals, and what has been written is always seen from an outsider's point of view, and not from the point of view of the person involved.

Over the history of modern civilisation emerged a number of charismatic people that seemingly perform tasks with the ease and wonder of a supernatural person. They reach into situations and transform evil into good, frustration into excitement and despair into hope. Great political leaders, artists, musicians, and even magicians. Though the approaches they bring to this task seem to vary, they all seem to share a unique skill of knowing what to say and what to do to influence.

It could be said that these achievers had an enormous personal presence and willingness to risk going wherever his or her intuitive feelings took them and had a profound capacity to be in touch with anyone who worked with them or around them. So brilliant is their intuition and so powerful are their approaches to situations that sometimes it took only seconds or minutes to make a major decision to avert a war or become rich beyond many people's wildest dreams.

These people seem to have a magical quality. To deny this power or to simply label it as a born talent, or genius is to limit our potential. For by doing this, one disregards the opportunity to learn, or to offer to people, an experience that they may use to change their lives and to enjoy its fullness.

The aim of this new learning approach is not to question the talent and skill of these achievers, but rather to show that this special task which they perform. This is just like other complex human activities such as learning to walk, learning languages, painting, or composing music, has a structure and therefore can be learned, given the right resources. By learning how to learn you will able to do so. You will be presented with a set of tools, so that you may improve, and enrich, the skills you already have. This set of tools is based upon human processes that are represented in the form of a learning model.

Scholars and practitioners have made the point that there is a major difference between the world and our experience of it, for we do not operate directly on it. Each of us creates a representation of the world in which we live; we create a model, which we use to generate behaviour. Our model of the world determines what our experience of the world would be, how we understand the world, and what choices we make. Following from that, no two human beings have exactly the same experiences of the world, for each of us would create a different representation of the world and thus would live in their own reality.

It is important to note that, the model is not the world and that the model varies from one person to another, but the main influencing factors are either internal or external but can be classified further by being also personal, that is, influenced by our own belief or value system.

Internal: If you consider the five human senses, hearing, seeing, feeling, tasting, and smelling, and their limitations, then there are some processes that could be considered beyond the limits of these senses. For example, certain sound or light spectrums, and the frequencies included in these spectrums that cannot be seen or heard, whereas they could be if you were an animal or an insect. Similarly, the human body is sensitive to touch. In an experiment conducted, it was established that a simple experience can create different feelings within us depending on the area of the skin touched, and therefore a range of real-world simulated situations could be interpreted as a completely different experience depending on the response of the person's internal nervous system. So although our physical world stays the same, our experience of that world might change, due to our nervous system that might delete and distort some or all of our perception of the real world. This would thus limit our experience possibilities, through its genetic filters.

External: The second factor in which our representation of the world differs from the physical world itself is through environmental and social constraints to which we are subject to as members of a social system. This includes our language, our accepted ways of behaving, and all the socially agreed upon rules, which again differ from one society to another. But the most recognised socially influencing factor is the language systems.

While human beings are capable of making millions of different colour distinctions in the visible colour spectrum, linguistically speaking there are only eight colours that are described in the English language. Other societies group their experience into fewer categories as restricted by their language that cover the same range of their physical sensation which the eight colours described in English do. This restriction in or variety in the case of an English language speaker provides a range of perceived distinctions, in describing the same real world. And unlike our nervous filters and our genetic restrictions, the environmental or social restrictions can be easily overcome by introducing other symbols or by speaking more than one language, and therefore we can use more than one set of tools to describe our experiences.

So these experiences which we share with other members of the same environment, are another way in which our models of the world differ from the world itself. Although the neurological system is the same for all human beings, and the social and environmental filters are, in general, the same for the members of the same linguistic community, there are many different linguistic communities, and thus this set of filters begins to distinguish us as human beings. Our experiences become more radically different, changing our representation of the same physical world.

Personal: The third set of factors; the personal factors are the most influencing differences among human beings. This refers to all the created representations based on our personal experiences, for every person has a set of experiences which is his own personal record of their life. The same way every person has a set of distinct physical characteristics, so, too, does each person has his own personal experiences of developing, growing up and simply living, and no two life experiences are identical though they may have similarities. The representations that we create in the course of our lives are based on our individual unique experiences. In these personal ways, each of us represents the world grouped as a set of likes, dislikes, habits, and preferences that are distinctly our own and are strongly influenced by our belief system.

What is important to highlight is that beliefs are not based on a logical frame of ideas, but instead are intended to coincide with reality, and since reality is personal and necessarily communal, you might form a belief as a matter of faith.

In modelling experiences, it should be remembered that it is not that the world is too limited or that there are no choices, but that people either limit their choices or stop themselves from seeing those options and possibilities that are open to them since they are not available in their restricted models.

Every human being in his life cycle has phases of change and transition, which he must go through. Some people can negotiate these periods of change with little difficulty, experiencing through these phases' intense energy and creativity. Others faced with the same situations, experience pain, and anguish. The main difference between these two types of people is that one responds positively by creating opportunities and changing the situation into a challenge, whereas the others would get stuck and possibly go nowhere. They experience themselves as having few options, none of which are attractive to them. So how is it possible for different people faced with the same world have different experiences?

This difference follows from differences in their models. They are making the best choices from what they believe is available to them that is available in their particular model.

Human behaviour always makes sense when it is seen in the context of the choices generated by their model.

The paradox of the human condition is that the processes which allow us to survive and adapt, and experience happiness and fulfilment are the same processes which allow us to keep the same restricted model of the world. The same processes that allow us to achieve high goals are the same processes, which stop our natural development by wrongly assuming that our representational system, our model of the world, is reality.

Preparing for Change: We are changing all the time but sometimes we embrace the change and sometimes we are reluctant to move on. What we become, what we do and what we accomplish in life is the product of how we respond to changes that we encounter. Our response to change is governed by the way we think, our belief systems, our attitudes and our expectations.

Accepting change is fundamental to our growth and development for whatever age we have reached we are continuously learning. A positive attitude about change will increase our capacity of learning and change for the better.

Change is natural. The stages of change are:

 The change process will start at the <u>Acceptance</u> stage when we are prepared to face reality.

At this stage there is true recognition that the old way is not for us anymore. At this stage we accept the need for change and commit to meaningful goals. As acceptance grows we start to experiment and try out new behaviours and test their appropriateness to the new situation. There is often a degree of frustration but is directed at not achieving our goals quickly. At the <u>Agreement</u> stage new strategies are tested and integrated within our belief system. The aim of is to move it into a conscious level and turn it into an ability to cope before placing this ability into the subconscious level again. This is when we complete the <u>Change</u> stage.

Most of our behaviour is habitual and is carried out without thinking, or subconsciously. Over 90 percent of our thinking and accordingly of our behaviour is subconscious to the point that for example in sport "thinking" becomes more about strategy and tactic than actual behaviour. Even highly intellectual or technical work can become habitual and routine driven after a certain period of time. This automatic pilot facility that we all possess is the main resource that we individuals have and need for achieving a better outcome and ultimately excellence. It is what we call subconscious competence, which is the ultimate level of learning and eventually changing. It has four stages.

Subconscious Incompetence or subconscious ignorance, is the state of mind in which we are not aware of a certain limitation or lack of skill or actual accumulated knowledge or skill or talent. Unless we map this stage and bring it up to the level of consciousness, we will not be able to learn new things.

Conscious Incompetence or conscious ignorance is the state of mind that is very important to our learning process, for it opens up the possibilities, opportunities, understandings, and skills. Although most adults claim to be wise, knowledgeable and experts in their fields of knowledge, mainly due to their repetitive exposure to the same events in their business life, social interests or hobbies, they do not use the same knowledge and skills in handling new challenges in their lives.

Conscious competence. This is the state of being we can reach by learning and training. Most of us have something that we are good at even if its outcome is negative and does not improve our lives or those of others.

Conscious competence. This is the most important stage in terms of learning, improving our lives and driving towards excellence. There are many activities, physical or otherwise that we carry out without thinking, that are complex in their contents. The competence involved is, usually measured by others remarking on the fact that we do these activities well. A non-swimmer or non-driver appreciate the achievement of swimming or driving whereas we would take it for granted. Similar comparisons could be made with people who are artistic, or good at music or arithmetic. Such people do not usually know what the fuss is all about because their competence is mainly habitual and is at a subconscious level. They do not think about their achievements consciously, for if they did, they would probably have difficulty achieving the same level of competence and start considering consciously the complexity of the activity. This is exactly the opposite to what a child would do without an adult social judgment system that puts him in a state of mind that could set him up to fail.

This is mainly because the conscious mind can only handle few things at a time. In a learning state, we are conscious of not being able to remember everything at the same time, whether driving a car, playing a musical instrument, or operating a computer. Only with repetition do we become competent, and improve with further practice till we perform the activity subconsciously.

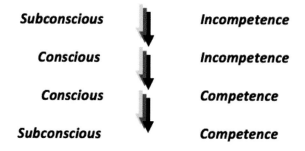

Subconscious   **Incompetence**

Conscious   **Incompetence**

Conscious   **Competence**

Subconscious   **Competence**

In changing for the better, the person or the organization must know what 'for the better means' so it could be measured and verified by all concerned. There must be a goal or a set of goals for without a goal or a desired outcome, the change in behaviour might be futile and at best not motivated enough to achieve the highest level desired.
Behaviour can only be successful against some criteria that could be defined as a plan of action, or technically defined as a strategy for change. Most of us look at planning as an investment in time believing that by planning we can get things done better and more smoothly.

Preparing for change requires a 'how to' strategy', a very important element of which is to get the person involved into the right state. The goal or outcome in this instance is invariably a package, including how he feels, or the state that he is in, as well as what he wants to achieve in a physical or material sense. These related or implicit roles and intentions may not be stated or consciously set, or formally identified. But they would affect your success, so the sooner you identify them, the better.

Experiencing Change: The steps that are necessary for any effective change strategy are the ones that drive you forward, stops you from going back, empowers you with the resources that you need and raises your receptors so that you operate subconsciously at a higher level of sensory awareness. This is what we call the Cycle of Excellence:

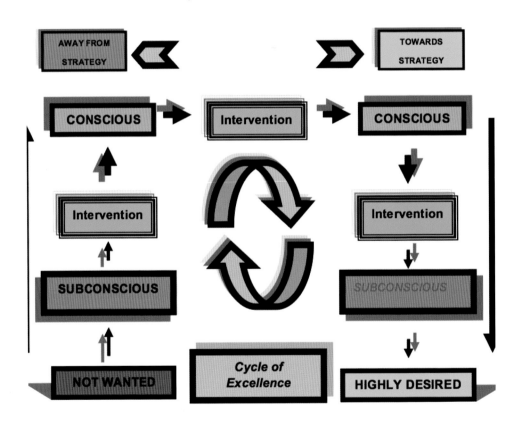

The steps that are necessary for any effective change strategy are the ones that drive you forward, stops you from going back, empowers you with the resources that you need and raises your receptors so that you operate subconsciously at a higher level of sensory awareness. This is what we call the Cycle of Excellence

Goal Setting and Achieving the Desired Outcomes: The importance of goal setting is to identify the changes that you want to make in your life, and the goals you want to achieve. The difference between a goal and an outcome is that a goal is a statement of intent of a requirement or a desire about some aspect in the future. Goals usually start with the word I want to be followed by a description of what is wanted to happen. An outcome, on the other hand, is a result whose success or failure could be measured. There are sensory experiences associated with that outcome defined by the way you see, hear or feel when that outcome is achieved. It is very important to recognise the difference between the two directly related events by recognising that a goal is usually set at a conscious level whereas a desired outcome is more perceived on a subconscious level.

Breaking the main goal into sub goals will help "agreeing" the outcome more clearly and will define ways of how it could be achieved better. Writing the goals gives the person involved a point of focus and a strategy of going towards something and not going away from something else. By seeing the outcome, the person involved will get into that state of mind that will make him experience that outcome as if it has happened already. As with any process repeating it continuously will move it as a fact from the conscious level to the subconscious level so that the mind will not differentiate whether it can be done or not but accepts that it will be.

Misconceptions about the way the brain operates are embedded in corporate training programs and could be sabotaging their effectiveness. Companies should re-evaluate them in light of the latest scientific insights.

Over the years, you have probably gained some insight into how your brain works. You may have taken a course or read a book that promised to reveal the secret of maximizing your mental capacity—a common sales pitch of leadership coaches these days. In the process, you may have read that after a critical period in childhood there is no hope for significant learning, that half of your brain is inactive at any given time, or that you're capable of learning properly only in your preferred style. Each of these claims is what we call a "neuro-myth," a misconception based on incorrect interpretations of neuroscientific research. Our experience advising companies on their lifelong-learning initiatives suggests that such misunderstandings remain embedded in many corporate training programs. As companies increasingly pour money into developing their employees, they can no longer afford to invest in training programs based on inaccurate and out-of-date assumptions. In recent years, for example, US businesses alone spent more than $164 billion annually on employee learning.

Bridging the gap between popular neuro-myths and the scientific insights gathered in the past few decades is a growing challenge. As modern brain-imaging techniques, such as functional magnetic resonance imaging (fMRI), have scientific advanced, these misleading lay interpretations by business practitioners have advanced as well. Unless such misconceptions are eliminated, they will continue to undermine both personal- and organizational-learning efforts.

THE CRITICAL WINDOW OF CHILDHOOD

Most of us have read about critical learning periods—the first years of life when the vast majority of the brain's development is thought to occur. After this period human development is deemed to be more or less fixed. That, however, is an exaggeration. Recent research indicates that experience can change both the brain's physical structure and its functional organization—a phenomenon described as neuroplasticity.

Researchers studying the plasticity of the brain are increasingly interested in mindfulness. Practicing simple meditation techniques, such as concentrated breathing, helps build denser gray matter in parts of the brain associated with learning and memory, controlling emotions, and compassion. A team led by Harvard scientists has shown that just eight weeks of mindful meditation can produce structural brain changes significant enough to be picked up by MRI scanners.

Organizations from General Mills in consumer foods to digital bellwethers such as Facebook and Google increasingly give their employees opportunities to benefit from mindfulness and meditation. Most such programs have garnered enthusiastic support from employees, who often see a marked improvement in their mind-sets and job performance. For example, employees at the health insurer Aetna who have participated in the company's free yoga and meditation classes report, on average, a 28 percent decrease in their levels of stress and a productivity increase of 62 minutes a week—an added value of approximately $3,000 per employee a year.

More leaders understand that providing them with the tools to become more focused and mindful can foster a better working environment conducive to development and high performance.

THE IDLE-BRAIN THEORY

A recent European survey discovered that nearly 50 percent of teachers surveyed in the United Kingdom and the Netherlands believed that the idle-brain theory had been proved scientifically. This misunderstanding originally stemmed from inaccurate interpretations of activation hot spots in brain-imaging studies. By now, more carefully interpreted functional brain scans have shown that, irrespective of what a person is doing, the entire brain is generally active and that, depending on the task, some areas are more active than others. People can always learn new ideas and new skills, not by tapping into some unused part of the brain, but by forming new or stronger connections between nerve cells. This insight into the brain's capacity becomes particularly relevant for the environment and context in which learning typically occurs. Everybody knows, all too well, about the habit of quickly checking e-mails or planning for the next meeting in the middle of a training session. The problem is that such multitasking engages large parts of the brain's working memory. Without freeing that up, we cannot successfully memorize and learn new information. In short, multitasking and learning cannot occur effectively at the same time.

LEARNING STYLES AND THE LEFT / RIGHT BRAIN HYPOTHESIS

Almost everyone has encountered the theory that most people are either dominantly analytical (and left brained) or more creative (and right brained). However, this either/or dichotomy is false. The two hemispheres of the brain are linked and communicate extensively together; they do not work in isolation. The simplistic notion of a false binary has led, in many businesses, to the misconception that each one of us has a strictly preferred learning style and channel. Recent studies have flatly disproved this idea, suggesting instead that engaging all the senses in a variety of ways (for instance, audiovisual and tactile) can help employees retain new content.

KFC – Customer Service as a Game

One organization that puts this idea into practice is KFC, which uses multiple forms of learning in customer-service training. Sessions begin with an after-hours board game plaacing the entire team of a store in the role of the customer. This is followed up by "gamified" learning that fits into roughly 15-minute windows during shifts. These video game–like modules put the employees behind the cash register to handle a number of typical customer experiences, including responding to audio and visual cues of satisfaction. At the end of the online modules, employees physically reconvene at the front of the store to hear feedback, report on what they've learned, and receive live coaching as reinforcement.

CHAPTER 4

Humanizing the Organization

Intelligent organizations provide work environments that are open to creative thought and embrace the concept that solutions to ongoing work-related problems are available inside every one of us. To succeed, they must tap into the knowledge base, which gives their staff the "ability to think critically and creatively, the ability to communicate ideas and concepts, and the ability to cooperate with other human beings in the process of inquiry and action

Like an intelligent human, an intelligent organization seeks to determine its future; that assumes learning and adaptation is an ongoing and creative process for its members; and one that develops, adapts, and transforms itself in response to the needs and aspirations of people, both inside and outside of itself.

What intelligent organizations do is set their human capital. Employees no longer have to be passive players in the equation; they learn to express ideas and challenge themselves to contribute to an improved work environment by participating in a shift from the traditional authoritarian workplace philosophy to one where the hierarchy is broken down, and human potential is heralded. They foster an environment wherein people can "create the results they truly desire," and where they can learn to learn together for the betterment of the whole.

Five disciplines that must be mastered when introducing learning into an organization:

1.   Systems Thinking: The ability to see the big picture, and to distinguish patterns instead of conceptualizing change as isolated events. There must be a paradigm shift - from being unconnected to interconnected to the whole, and from blaming problems on something external to a realization that how we operate, our actions, our approach and especially our thinking, can create problems.

2.	Personal Beliefs of wanting to improve: Being committed to lifelong dynamic learning is the spiritual cornerstone of an individual organization.

3.	Existing Belief Systems: Must be managed because they prevent new powerful insights and organizational practices from becoming implemented. The process begins with self-reflection; unearthing deeply held belief structures and generalizations, and understanding how they influence the way we operate in our own lives. Until there is realization and a focus on openness, real change can never take place.

4.	Building Shared Visions based on supporting beliefs: Visions cannot be dictated because they always begin with the personal visions of individual employees, who may not agree with the leader's vision. What is needed is a genuine collective vision that elicits commitment in good times and bad, and has the power to bind an organization together.

5.	Team Learning: Important because modern organizations operate on the basis of teamwork, which means that organizations cannot learn if team members do not come together and learn. It is a process of developing the ability to create desired results; to have a goal in mind and work together to attain it.

An intelligent organization does away with the militaristic hierarchical mindset that it is only senior management who can and do all the thinking for an entire corporation. It challenges all employees to tap into their inner resources and potential, in the hope that they can build their own community based on principles of liberty, humanity, and a collective will to learn.

To compete in the information-saturated environment that we are currently living in it is necessary to remain dynamic, competitive, and to continue to look for ways to improve organizations.

As David Garvin of Harvard University writes, "continuous improvement requires a commitment to learning." Change is the only constant we should expect in the workplace, and therefore, we must rid ourselves of traditional, hierarchal organizational structures that are often change-averse, or undergo change only as a reaction to external events. Intelligent learning organizations embrace change and constantly create reference points to precipitate an ever-evolving structure that has a vision of the future built-in. Learning organizations are healthier places to work because they:

- Nourish Independent Thinking
- Enable Staff to Manage Change
- Stretch and Ultimately Remove Perceived Limits
- Believe in The Need to Learn, To Improve, To Act

The very first thing needed to create a learning organization is effective leadership, which is not based on a traditional hierarchy, but rather, is a mix of different people from all levels of the system, who lead in different ways.

Secondly, there must be a realization that we all have the inherent power to find solutions to the problems we are faced with, and that we can and will envision a future and forge ahead to create it. An intelligent learning organization's culture is based on openness and trust, where employees are supported and rewarded for learning and innovating, and one that promotes experimentation, risk-taking, and values the well-being of all employees.

To create a culture and environment that will act as the foundation for a learning organization begins with a shift of mind - from seeing ourselves as separate from the world to connect to the world; seeing ourselves as integral components in the workplace, rather than as separate and unimportant cogs in a wheel. Finally, one of the biggest challenges that must be overcome in any organization is to identify and breakdown the ways people reason defensively. Until then, change can never be anything but a passing phase. Everyone must learn that the steps they use to define and solve problems can be a source of additional problems for the organization.

The first step is to create a timeline to initiate the types of changes necessary to achieve the principles of a learning organization.

One: Create a communications system to facilitate the exchange of information, the basis on which any learning organization is built.

The use of technology has and will continue to alter the workplace by enabling information to flow freely and to provide universal access to business and strategic information. It is also important in clarifying the more complex concepts into more precise language that is understandable across departments.

Two: Organize a readiness process that assesses the distance between where an organization is and where it would like to be, in terms of the following seven dimensions - Providing continuous learning, providing strategic leadership, promoting inquiry and dialogue, encouraging collaboration and team learning, creating embedded structures for capturing and sharing learning, empowering people toward a shared vision, and making systems connections. The process is administered by all employees or a sample of them and is used to develop an assessment profile to design the learning organization initiative.

Three: Commit to developing, maintaining, and facilitating an atmosphere that garners learning and creates a vision of the organization and writes a mission statement with the help of all employees.

Four: Use training and awareness programs to develop skills and understanding attitudes that are needed to reach the goals of the mission statement, including the ability to work well with others, become more verbal, and network with people across all departments within the organization.

Five: Communicate a change in the company's culture by integrating human and technical systems and initiate emphasizing team learning and contributions. Employees will become more interested in self-regulation and management, and be more prepared to meet the challenges of an ever-changing workplace. Allow employees to question key business practices and assumptions and develop workable expectations for future actions.

CHAPTER 5

The Engineering of Intelligent Leadership

What sort of leadership behavior intelligent organizations should encourage. Is leadership so contextual that it defies standard definitions or development approaches?

This consuming interest in leadership and how to make it better has created an industry of gurus whose wisdoms are often completely disconnected from organizational reality and, as a consequence, useless for sparking an intelligent, productive and integrated working culture. Estimates of the amount spent on leadership training range from $14 billion to $50 billion a year in the United States alone. An amount equivalent to the GDP of a small nation that already functions very well.

The first most obvious problem is that thinking on leadership has become a sort of morality tale. There are some who advocate authenticity, attention to employees' well-being, telling the truth, building trust, being agreeable, and so on. A smaller number of empirical researchers, contrarily, report evidence on the positive effects of traits and behavior such as narcissism, self-promotion, rule-breaking, lying, and shrewd maneuvering on salaries, getting jobs, accelerating career advancement, and projecting an aura of power. The main reason of this big gap in agreement on the definition and expectations between the prescriptions of the vast leadership industry and the data on what in actuality produces career success, stems from the unacknowledged tendency to confuse what people believe ought to be true with what in reality is. Underlying that is an associated bias: the tendency to see, and remember, what you are motivated to believe.

An essay on the 500th anniversary of the writing of Machiavelli's The Prince by John T. Scott and Robert Zaretsky, "Why Machiavelli still matters," New York Times, December 9, 2013, noted that it is sometimes necessary to do bad things to achieve good results. Not surprisingly, then, some of the most successful and admired leaders—for example, Nelson Mandela, Abraham Lincoln, and John F. Kennedy—

Learn Intelligently or Die – Psychopathy in Business

Traditionally thought of as being egocentric and lacking in empathy, psychopaths might be assumed unlikely to prosper in collaborative business environments, but in many cases, they thrive. They are charismatic and adept at manipulating one-on-one interactions. The seminal work on the subject is "Snakes in Suits – When Psychopaths Go To Work" by Paul Babiak and Robert Hale (2006). Studies have shown that in senior management positions over 3% of people are on the psychopathy scale compared with just 1% in the general population.

were above all pragmatists, willing to do what was necessary to achieve important objectives.

As such, each of them (and many other renowned leaders) changed their positions on decisions and issues and behaved inconsistently. They dissembled and engaged in strategic misrepresentation, not always disclosing their full agendas and plans, in part to avoid provoking opposition. At times, they acted in ways inconsistent with their authentic feelings. Human beings are complex and multidimensional, so not only do bad people do good things and vice versa, but the whole idea of good and evil can also be problematic when you consider the knotty dilemmas leaders face deciding whether the ends justify the means.

Finally, the division of leaders and their actions into good and evil oversimplifies a much more complex reality and continues to reinforce a problematic, trait-based, and personality-centric view of human behavior. As social-psychological research has made clear for decades, people are not only shaped by their enduring traits but are also profoundly influenced by cues and constraints that vary by situation. So they adopt different types of behavior and even personas, depending on the circumstances and the various roles they play. To take one example, leaders may behave differently within their families and religious institutions than they do at work. When individuals are promoted to management, their perspectives change and so too does their behavior.

Research also suggests that the effectiveness of various types of leadership behavior varies with the health of the organization in which they are practiced. Characterizing leaders' behavior as somehow dependent on inherent traits provides an easy excuse for avoiding the sort of behavior and strategies that may be required to get things done. Humans were not born walking, they learned how to do so.

The most important message embodied in all of these leaders is their capacity to get things done. It is a skill that can be improved like any other, from playing a musical instrument or speaking a foreign language to mastering a sport. The leaders highlighted above, and others like them evolved and developed over time. They learned how to weigh what trade-offs they were willing to make and, more important, to size up the circumstances required to achieve their bold objectives.

In so doing, they illustrate what could be possible for those who willingly step into the arena to tackle important, and therefore contested, problems. More critically, they are a caution against self-handicapping and a reluctance to embrace required types of behavior—deficiencies that keep many leaders from living up to their full potential

New research suggests that the secret to developing effective leaders is to encourage four types of behavior.

Solving problems effectively. The process that precedes decision making is problem-solving when information is gathered, analyzed, and considered. This is deceptively difficult to get right, yet it is a key input into decision making for major issues (such as M&A) as well as daily ones (such as how to handle a team dispute).

Operating with a strong results orientation. Leadership is about not only developing and communicating a vision and setting objectives but also following through to achieve results. Leaders with a strong results orientation tend to emphasize the importance of efficiency and productivity and to prioritize the highest-value work.

Seeking different perspectives. This trait is conspicuous in managers who monitor trends affecting organizations, grasp changes in the environment, encourage employees to contribute ideas that could improve performance, accurately differentiate between important and unimportant issues, and give the appropriate weight to stakeholder concerns. Leaders who do well on this dimension typically base their decisions on prudent analysis and avoid the many biases to which decisions are prone.

Supporting others. Leaders who are supportive understand and sense how other people feel. By showing authenticity and a sincere interest in those around them, they build trust and inspire and help colleagues to overcome challenges. They intervene in group work to promote organizational efficiency, allaying unwarranted fears about external threats and preventing the energy of employees from dissipating into internal conflict.

We're not saying that the centuries-old debate about what distinguishes great leaders is over or that context is unimportant. Experience shows that different business situations often require different styles of leadership. We do believe, however, that our research points to a kind of core leadership behavior that will be relevant to most companies today, notably on the front line. For organizations investing in the development of their future leaders, prioritizing these four areas is a good place to start.

The short stories on the pages ahead are example of Intelligent Learning in practice.

Defy the Odds: The story of Lech Walesa

Labor activist and later Polish President Lech Walesa helped form and lead communist Poland's first independent trade union, Solidarity and won a Nobel Prize. Lech Walesa was born September 29, 1943, in Popowo, Poland. He helped form and led (1980–1990) communist Poland's first independent trade union, Solidarity. The charismatic leader of millions of Polish workers, he went on to become the President of Poland (1990–1995). He received the Nobel Prize for Peace in 1983. He ran for President again in 2000 but carried only a tiny fraction of the vote.

Change the Rules: The Story of Margaret Thatcher

The first female Prime Minister of Britain, Margaret Thatcher was a controversial figurehead of conservative ideology during her time in office. Her famous quote was "One of the things being in politics has taught me is that men are not a reasoned or reasonable sex."

Margaret Thatcher was the first female Prime Minister of the United Kingdom. Her speech against communism earned her the name "The Iron Lady." Leading Britain through a war and out of a recession, she left a huge mark on politics.

Born on October 13, 1925, in Grantham, England, Margaret Thatcher became Britain's Conservative Party leader and in 1979 was elected prime minister, the first woman to hold the position. During her three terms, she cut social welfare programs, reduced trade union power and privatized certain industries. Thatcher resigned in 1991 due to unpopular policy and power struggles in her party. She died on April 8, 2013, at age 87.

Create a Ruthless Popular Image: The Story of Steve Jobs

There is little doubt that Steve Jobs was, on the one hand, a visionary leader who co-founded and built an amazingly successful company, Apple—and helped build another, Pixar—and, on the other, was notoriously hard on the people who worked for and with him. The takeaway: leadership is not about winning popularity contests or being the most beloved person in a social organization. Creating things and innovating often disturb the status quo and vested interests. Moreover, the monomaniacal focus and energy so useful in bringing great ideas to life are not always pleasant for those nearby.

Plan Change: The Story of Sheikh Mohammed Bin Rashid of Dubai

Sheikh Mohammed Bin Rashid is the ruler of a small sheikhdom situated on the Arabian Gulf and part of United Arab Emirates. He is also the Prime Minister of the UAE. In ten years he has reinvented Dubai as a center of excellence and one of the top destinations for travelers. Emirates Airline is the most successful airline in the world, Palm Jumeirah is a worldwide development seen from outer space, and the Burj Khalifa is the tallest building on earth.

In his ten years of governance, Sheikh Mohammed bin Rashid managed to raise the standard of the government's competitiveness internationally by establishing institutions and work teams that focus on satisfying citizens and making them happy. In 2013 his highness launched Dubai Smart Government Establishment (DSGE), an initiative to provide innovative Smart government services to all sections of society. In the same year, Dubai won the right to host the World Expo in Dubai in 2020. This will be the first time that the World Expo will be staged in the Middle East, North Africa and South Asia. In 2014 the Government announced the launch of the "Happiness Meter" making Dubai the first city in the world to measure its visitors and residents' happiness interactively. In 2015, the Government announced the establishment of a new Space Centre. It's mission is to support the UAE's efforts in the space field with the launch of Al Amal ('Hope'), the Arab world's first Mars probe. By establishing an integrated infrastructure to manufacture the satellite in the UAE, this will take advantage of its applications in all areas of technological development.

Setting Goals and Standards: Virtues of the Island City State of Singapore

Singapore is one of the most successful societies in modern history. No country has improved the living standards of its people faster and with more impact, rising from third world status in 1965 when it separated from Malaysia. It grew with a per capita income of $500 to arguably becoming the most advanced nation on earth where it's development and living standards now overshadow its former colonizers and the US and Europe.

How did Singapore succeed and what can be learned? The shortest possible answer is the M-P-H policy: Meritocracy, Pragmatism, and Honesty. Singapore's founding prime minister Lee Kuan Yew implemented First, choose the best people for the job, not family and friends! Secondly, be pragmatic. No matter what problem, somebody, somewhere, has solved it. Copy the solution and adapt it. And finally, "Honesty." Whether a developing nation or a leading industry organization, corruption is a latent virus that is always at risk to corrode and break down countries and companies alike. What we can learn from Singapore is identifying the standard you want to live up and not compromising on the resources and work needed to reach and maintain it.

CHAPTER 6

Intelligent Strategy

Elements of Success

The new disruptive patterns discussed earlier gathered pace, grew in scale, and started collectively to have a material impact on the world economy around the turn of the 21st century. Today, they are disrupting long-established patterns in virtually every market and every sector of the world economy—indeed, in every aspect of our lives.

Everywhere we look, they are causing trends to break down, to break up, or simply to break. The fact that all four are happening at the same time means that our world is changing radically from the one in which many of us grew up, prospered, and formed the intuitions that are so vital to our decision making.

This can play havoc with forecasts and pro forma plans that were made simply by extrapolating recent experience into the near and distant future. Many of the assumptions, tendencies, and habits that had long proved so reliable have suddenly lost much of their resonance. We have never had more data and advice at our fingertips—literally. The iPhone or the Samsung Galaxy contains far more information and processing power than the original supercomputer, and earlier simple mobile phones had more processing capacity than NASA when it sent a man to the moon. However, we work in a world in which even, perhaps especially, professional forecasters are routinely caught unawares. That is partly because intuition still underpins much of our decision making.

Our intuition has been formed by a set of experiences and ideas about how things worked during a time when changes were incremental and somewhat predictable.

Globalization benefited the well-established and well connected, opening up new markets with relative ease. Labor markets functioned quite reliably. Resource prices fell. But that is not how things are working now—and it is not how they are likely to work in the future. If we look at the world through a rearview mirror and make decisions on the basis of the intuition built on our experience, we could well be wrong. In the new world, executives, policymakers, and individuals all need to scrutinize their intuitions from first principles and boldly reset them if necessary. This is especially true for organizations that have enjoyed great success.

While it is full of opportunities, this era is deeply unsettling. And there is a great deal of work to be done. We need to realize that much of what we think we know about how the world works is wrong; to get a handle on the disruptive forces transforming the global economy; to identify the long-standing trends that are breaking; to develop the courage and foresight to clear the intellectual decks and prepare to respond. These lessons apply as much to policy makers as to business executives, and the process of resetting your internal navigation system cannot begin soon enough.

It is imperative to adjust to these new realities. For all the ingenuity, inventiveness, and imagination of the human race, we tend to be slow to adapt to change. There is a powerful human tendency to want the future to look much like the recent past. It is axiomatic that most armies are perfectly configured to fight the last war.

Revisiting our assumptions about the world we live in—and doing nothing—will leave many of us highly vulnerable. Gaining a clear-eyed perspective on how to negotiate the changing landscape will help us prepare to succeed.

Uncertainty and rising levels of risk make it impossible for companies to determine the future. But a portfolio-of-initiatives approach to strategy can help ensure that companies take full advantage of their best opportunities without taking unnecessary risks.

The classic approach to corporate strategy starts with a presumption: that with sufficient analytical rigor and an adequate assessment of the probabilities, strategists can pave a predictable path to the future from the experience of the past.

In this world, they make reasonable assumptions about the evolution of product markets, capital markets, technology, and government regulation and, in effect, "assume away" most risk.

Such traditional strategy formulation often pays lip service to the perspectives of the capital markets, to changing industry structures, and to the forces at work in the environment.

So suppose we no longer believe that the future is foreseeable. What if defining and achieving an enduring competitive advantage is really just a conceit that must be abandoned? What if it is no longer possible to block out the "noise" of the world's messy reality in order to rationalize a plan to achieve predetermined outcomes?

In fact, this is the confusing, complex, and uncertain environment that corporate leaders now face. Globalization and technology are sweeping away the market and industry structures that have historically defined the nature of competition.

Although the pace of change continues to accelerate, the fundamental transformations underway in the global economy have only just started. Only 20 percent of the world's GDP comes from industries that can be called global. It will take 30 years or more before anything reasonably approaching a truly integrated global economy will be realized. Over the intervening period, the world's market and industry structures will be in continuous flux. The variables that can profoundly influence success and failure are too numerous to count. That makes it impossible to predict, with any confidence, which markets a company will be serving or how its industry will be structured—even a few years from now.

The result is an economic environment that is rich in opportunity but also marked by a substantial increase in awareness of risk and aversion to it— a phenomenon reflected in the rise of risk premiums throughout the world even while the risk-free cost of capital remains low.

Strategy for Success

Strategy today has to align itself with the fluid nature of this external environment. It must be flexible enough to change constantly and to adapt to outside and internal conditions even as the aspiration to deliver favorable outcomes for shareholders remains constant.

The new strategy function is a tag team that combines mainly the CEO and the CFO; creating a new leadership function - the Corporate Command and Control Center or the C Center or C4.

The C Center can think about corporate strategy not as a "portfolio of businesses" but as a "portfolio of initiatives" aimed at achieving favorable outcomes for the entire enterprise. Usually, these initiatives will be organized around themes—"convoys" if you please—focused on achieving particular aspirations, such as increasing the global reach of the enterprise, entering a new but related industry, or achieving the industry's lowest marginal cost of production. Portfolio effects increase the likelihood that some of these aspirations will be achieved even if many others fail.

Like a more traditional strategy, such an effort is best led by an activist C Center, making use of the combined knowledge and command over talent and resources.

Think Intelligently or Die - The Convoy System

Consider the management problem of moving supplies and ships across the Pacific Ocean during World War II. The starting point for the strategist was to recognize that controlling the environment—the weather in the Pacific—was beyond anyone's power. However, risks could be minimized, and schedules roughly set, by studying weather patterns and using navigational tools. The real challenge was considering factors beyond the natural forces, such as enemy submarines and ships and air attacks. These threats are analogous to corporate competitors with unknown capabilities and plans.

The strategist's answer is to deploy whole convoys with a mix of aircraft carriers, battleships, destroyers, escort ships, troop ships, and supply ships. Convoys improve the ability of each ship to cross the ocean and, crucially, helped to ensure, through the "portfolio effects" of diversification, that sufficient supplies make it across the sea even though some ships will not. The strategist does know where battles will occur or exactly which ships he will lose to enemy fire. Nonetheless, the probability of success for individual vessels, and for the mission as a whole, is increased.

CHAPTER 7

Measuring Success and Value

Definition: Success is the accomplishment of an aim or purpose.

Anonyms: Failure, flop, disaster, nobody
It is disturbing that in a world that is continuously changing we judge lack of success as failure instead of encouraging experience to find out what works.

Companies, investors, and governments must relearn the guiding principles of value creation if they are to defend against future economic crises.

In response to the economic crisis that began in 2007, several thinkers argued that our ideas about market economies must change fundamentally if we are to avoid similar crises in the future. Questioning previously accepted financial theory, they promote a new model, with more explicit regulation that governs what companies and investors do, as well as new economic theories.

In my view, neither regulation nor new theories will prevent future bubbles or crises. This is because past ones have occurred largely when companies, investors, and governments have forgotten why investments succeed and how investments create value, how to measure value properly, or both. The result has been a misunderstanding about which investments are creating real value—a misunderstanding that persists until value-destroying investments have triggered a crisis. In the last crisis, even bankers believed their valuations which were faulty in its assumptions and unrealistic in its expectations. They assumed away risks by predicting how the world will change. This is the problem we are facing now; we cannot assume risk anymore.

Relearning how to create and measure value in the tried-and-true fashion is an essential step toward creating more secure economies and defending ourselves against future crises.

The main guiding principle of value creation is that companies create value by using capital they raise from investors to generate future cash flows at rates of return exceeding the cost of capital for cash is oxygen that businesses breathe and if it is not flowing freely, the whole organization will literally suffocate just like us, humans, when we are deprived of it.

The faster companies can increase their revenues and deploy more capital at attractive rates of return, the more value they create. The combination of growth and return on invested capital (ROIC) relative to its cost is what drives value. Companies can sustain strong growth and high returns on invested capital only if they have a well-defined competitive advantage. This is how competitive advantage, the core concept of business strategy, links to the guiding principle of value creation. This principle, known as the conservation of value, says anything that does not increase cash flows then it does not create value.

Economist Alfred Marshall spoke about the return on capital relative to the cost of capital in as early as 1890, yet we still choose to ignore it. The rise and fall of business conglomerates in the 1970s, hostile takeovers in the United States during the 1980s, the collapse of Japan's bubble economy in the 1990s, the Southeast Asian crisis in 1998, the dot-com bubble in the early 2000s, and the economic crisis starting in 2007 can all, to some extent, be traced to a misunderstanding or misapplication of these principles. With this knowledge, companies can make wiser strategic and operating decisions, such as what businesses to own and how to make trade-offs between growth and returns on invested capital—and investors can more confidently calculate the risks and returns of their investments. Thus be able to define value with less uncertainty.

Other companies like Amazon.com, eBay, and Yahoo!, have created and are likely to continue creating justified value. But for every solid, innovative, new business idea, there were dozens of companies that turned out to have virtually no ability to generate revenue or value in either the short or the long term.

Investors threw out fundamental rules of economics and assumed that in certain situations, as companies get bigger, they can earn higher margins and returns on capital because their product becomes more valuable with each new customer. In most industries, competition forces returns back to reasonable levels. But in industries with increasing returns, competition is kept at bay by the low and decreasing unit costs incurred by the market leader. It is like betting in casino expecting that your chances are great of playing the Roulette where the odds are 33 to 1 and forgetting that the odds of failure are 32 to 1.

Technology bubbles - Netscape

One of the many stories about the dot-com bubble is that of Netscape. When Netscape Communications went public in 1995, the company saw its market capitalization soar to $6 billion on an annual revenue base of just $85 million, a literally astonishing valuation. This phenomenon convinced the financial world that the Internet could change the way business was done and how value was created in every sector, setting off a race to create Internet-related companies and take them public. Between 1995 and 2000, more than 4,700 companies went public in the United States and Europe, many with billion-dollar-plus market capitalizations. Many of them disappeared when the bubble burst.

Microsoft

Microsoft's Office software is a product that provides word processing, spreadsheets, and graphics. As the number of Office users expanded, it became more attractive for new customers to follow suit to use the Office package. This is because of the superior compatibility of platforms for sharing documents, calculations, and images. Potential customers became increasingly unwilling to purchase and use competing products. Because of this advantage, Microsoft was making profit margins of more than 60 percent and roughly $12 billion a year on the Office package in 2009. This made it one of the most profitable products of all time, Microsoft one of the highest valued companies and its founder, Bill Gates, one of the wealthiest men on earth.

Microsoft's experience illustrates the strengths of the concept of increasing returns to scale. What was different for companies during the Internet era was the misapplication to almost every product and service related to the Internet. At that time, the concept was misinterpreted to mean that merely getting big faster than your competitors in a given market would result in enormous profits.

Microsoft was lucky because it acquired a monopoly position in the market thus demanding a high valuation.

However, the history of innovation during that era shows how difficult it is to earn monopoly-sized returns on capital for any length of time. The apparent conclusion seemed to be intentionally ignored.

The dot-com bubble left a sad trail of intellectual shortcuts taken to justify absurd prices for technology company shares. We call it the Starbucks Analysts Trading Investment Nuisance Strategy or SATIN's Strategy since it was probably invented by persons using Starbucks's free internet to trade online and pretending to understand market fundamentals. The Internet has revolutionized the economy, as have other innovations, but it did not, and could not render the rules of economics, competition, and value creation obsolete.

Financial Catastrophe

Behind the more recent financial and economic crises beginning in 2007 lies the fact that banks and investors forgot the principle of the conservation of value. First, individuals and speculators bought homes—illiquid assets, meaning they take a while to sell. They took out mortgages on which the interest was set at artificially low teaser rates for the first few years but then rose substantially when the teaser rates expired, and the required principal payments kicked in. In these transactions, the lender and buyer knew the buyer could not afford the mortgage payments after the teaser period ended. But both assumed either that the buyer's income would grow by enough that he or she could make the new payments or that the house's value would increase enough to induce a new lender to refinance the mortgage at similar, low teaser rates.

Banks packaged these high-risk debts into long-term securities and sold them to investors. The securities too were not very liquid, but the investors who bought them—typically hedge funds and other banks—used short-term debt to finance the purchase, thus creating a long-term risk for whoever lent them the money. They believed their faulty assumptions and in some cases as proven in court, they lied and believed their own lies.

When the interest rate on the home buyers' adjustable-rate debt increased, many could no longer afford the payments. Reflecting their distress, the real-estate market crashed, pushing the values of many homes below the values of the loans taken out to buy them. At that point, homeowners could neither make the required payments nor sell their houses. Seeing this, the banks that had issued short-term loans to investors in securities backed by mortgages became unwilling to roll over the loans, prompting the investors to sell all such securities at once. The value of the securities plummeted, and the whole financial system in the USA specifically fell like a house of cards.

This story reveals two fundamental flaws in the decisions made by participants in the securitized mortgage market that directly contradicts the principles of cash flows. They assumed that securitizing risky home loans made the loans more valuable because it reduced the risk of the assets. Securitizing the assets simply enabled their risks to be passed on to other owners who are the banks or the mortgage houses. The complexity of the chain of securities made it impossible to know who was holding precisely which risks. After the housing market crashed, financial-services companies feared that any of their counterparties could be holding massive risks and almost ceased to do business with one another. This was the start of the credit crunch that triggered a recession in the real economy.

The second flaw was to believe that using leverage to invest in itself creates value. It does not because it does not increase the cash flows from an investment. Many banks used large amounts of short-term debt to fund their illiquid long-term assets. This debt did not create long-term value for shareholders in those banks, on the contrary, it increased the risks of holding the equity in the bank because of increased liabilities.

Excessive borrowing on continuously conveniently revalued assets

Aggressive use of leverage is the theme that links most major financial crises. Companies, banks, or investors use short-term debt to buy long-term, illiquid assets. Typically, some event triggers unwillingness among lenders to refinance the short-term debt when it falls due, and since in some cases the borrowers do not have enough cash on hand to repay the short-term debt, they must sell some of their long-term assets. But because the assets are illiquid, and other borrowers are trying to do the same, the price each borrower can realize is too low to repay the debt. In other words, creating a situation where the borrower's assets and liabilities are mismatched.

The world in the last 30 years has seen at least six financial crises that arose largely because companies and banks were financing illiquid assets with short-term debt. During the 1980s, in the United States, savings-and-loan institutions funded an aggressive expansion with short-term debt and deposits. When it became clear that these institutions' investments were worth less than their liabilities, lenders and depositors refused to lend more to them. In 1989, the US government was forced to bail out the banks which again had implications on every aspect of the economy.

In the mid-1990s, the fast-growing economies in East Asia, including Indonesia, South Korea, and Thailand, fueled their investments in illiquid industrial property, plants, and equipment with short-term debt, often denominated in US dollars. When global interest rates rose, and it became clear that the East Asian companies had built too much capacity, those companies were unable to repay or refinance their debt. The ensuing crisis destabilized local economies and damaged foreign investors. As far as foreign investors were concerned, they pick up highly discounted assets that allowed the US and European companies to enter the Asian markets at highly discounted valuations.

Other financial crises fueled by too much short-term debt have included the Russian-government default and the collapse of the US hedge fund Long-Term Capital Management, both in 1998; the US commercial real-estate crisis of the early 1990s; and the Japanese financial crisis that began in 1990 and continues to this day.

Market bubbles and crashes are painfully disruptive, but we do not need new rules to avoid them. The key to avoiding the next crisis is to reassert the fundamental economic rules, not to revise them. If investors and lenders value their investments and loans according to the guiding principle of value creation, prices of assets will reflect the real risks underlying the transactions.

Stock Markets

For listed companies, the stock markets continue to reflect a company's intrinsic value during financial crises. The critical difference is that investors could easily trade shares on the equity markets, whereas credit markets (with the possible exception of the government bond market) are not nearly as liquid. Economic crises usually start from excesses in credit rather than equity markets.

The two types of markets, the stock markets, and the credit markets operate very differently. Equities are highly liquid because they trade on organized exchanges with many buyers and sellers for a relatively small number of securities. In contrast, there are many more debt securities than equities because there are often multiple debt instruments for each company and even more derivatives, many of which are not standardized or even understood by most borrowers or investors. Most of the debt is not traded at all. Short-term loans between banks and from banks to hedge funds are one-to-one transactions that are difficult to buy or sell. Illiquidity leads to frozen markets where no one will trade or where prices fall to levels far below that which reflect reasonable economic value.

During the credit crisis that began in 2007, prices on the equity markets became volatile, but for the most part, they operated normally. The volatility reflected the uncertainty hanging over the real economy. The S&P 500 index traded between 1,200 and 1,400 from January 2008 to September 2008. In October, upon the collapse of US investment bank Lehman Brothers and the US government takeover of the insurance company American International Group (AIG), the index began its

CHAPTER 8

Intelligent Learning Technologies

The new emerging technologies that include the mobile Internet, autonomous vehicles, and advanced genomics have the potential to truly reshape the world in which we live and work. Leaders in both government and business must not only know what is on the horizon but also start preparing for its impact. Going back to our advice to the world: Learn or Die!

The list of technologies that we believe will change the world include:

- Mobile Internet and Accessibility
- Automation of Knowledge
- Artificial Intelligence
- Cloud Storage and Analysis
- Advanced Robotics
- Autonomous Vehicles
- Next Generation Genomics
- Energy Storage
- 3-D Printing
- The Internet of Things

Not every emerging technology will alter the business or social landscape—but some truly do have the potential to change the status quo, alter the way people live and work, and rearrange our approach to value. It is therefore critical that business and policy leaders understand which technologies will matter to them and prepare accordingly.

The applications of those technologies could have a potential economic impact between $14 trillion and $33 trillion a year in 2025, compared with an estimated total value of the world economy of $77 trillion in 2014. It is based on an analysis of key potential applications and the value they could create in a number of ways, including the consumer surplus that arises from better products, lower prices, a cleaner environment, and better health.

Intelligent robotics — with enhanced cognitive dexterity, and intelligence—can take on tasks once thought too delicate or uneconomical to automate. These technologies can also generate significant benefits, including robotic surgical systems that make procedures less invasive, as well as robotic prosthetics.

Next-generation genomics marries the science used for imaging nucleotide base pairs (the units that make up DNA) with rapidly advancing computational and analytic capabilities. As our influence on the genomic makeup of humans increases, so does the ability to manipulate genes and improve health diagnostics and treatments. Genomics will offer similar advances in our understanding of plants and animals, potentially creating opportunities to improve the performance of agriculture and to create high-value substances—for instance, ethanol and biodiesel—from ordinary organisms, such as E. coli bacteria.

Energy-storage devices or physical systems store energy for later use. These technologies, such as lithium-ion batteries and fuel cells, already power electric and hybrid vehicles, along with billions of portable consumer electronics. Over the coming decade, advancing energy-storage technology could make electric vehicles cost competitive, and improve the efficiency of the utility grid thus moving the human race away from exhausting the energy resources of the earth that are being depleted at a catastrophic rate.

The potential benefits of these technologies are tremendous but not if business and government leaders wait until these technologies are exerting their full influence on the economy, for then it will be too late to capture the benefits or react to the consequences. As technological change accelerates and adoption rates soar, there are trends that should be closely monitored and understood by business leaders.

The pace of technology change, innovation, and business adoption since then has been stunning. The world's stock of data is now doubling every 20 months; the number of Internet-connected devices has reached 12 billion; and payments by mobile phone are hurtling toward the $1 trillion mark.

Big data and advanced analytics have swiftly moved to a set of capabilities that need to be deeply embedded across functions and operations, enabling managers to have a better basis for understanding markets and making business decisions. Meanwhile, social technologies are becoming a powerful social matrix—a key piece of organizational infrastructure that links and engages employees, customers, and suppliers as never before.

The Internet of Things (IoT), the linking of physical objects with embedded sensors, is being exploited at a breakneck pace, simultaneously creating massive network effects and opportunities. "The cloud," with its ability to deliver digital power at low cost and in small increments, is not only changing the profile of the corporate world but also helping to spawn a range of new business models by shifting the economics of "rent versus buy" trade-offs for companies and consumers.

The combined effect of these trends is an acceleration of business definition: the delivery of anything as a service. The slow adaptation of automation of knowledge, which affects the fastest-growing employee segment worldwide, promises a new phase of corporate productivity. Up to three billion new consumers, mostly in emerging markets, will soon become fully digital players, thanks to mobile technologies.

Research suggests that the collective economic impact of these technology applications could reach $20 trillion annually in 2025 and beyond.

The integration of digital and physical experiences is creating new ways for businesses to interact with customers, by using digital information to augment individual experiences with products and services. Consumer demand is rising for products that are free, intuitive, and radically user oriented. And the rapid evolution of cloud-enabled commerce is reducing entry barriers and opening new revenue streams to a range of individuals and companies.

These technological changes will also have direct effects on government, education, and healthcare—which often seem outside the purview of business leaders, they will have no choice but to adopt these digital technologies at the same level as many industries have. Productivity gains could help address the imperative (created by aging populations) to do more with less, while technological innovation could improve the quality and reach of many services. The embrace of digital technologies by these sectors is thus a trend of immense importance to business, which indirectly finances many services and would benefit greatly from the rising skills and improved health of citizens everywhere.

Data mines and advanced analytics

As with the social matrix, data mines and analytics will become a crucial part of global competitiveness. Global data volumes—surging from social Web sites, sensors, smartphones, and more—are doubling faster than ever. The power of analytics is rising while costs are falling. Data visualization, wireless communications, and cloud infrastructure are extending the power and reach of information.

With abundant data from multiple touch points and new analytic tools, companies are getting better and faster at customizing products and services through the creation of ever-finer consumer micro-segments. Companies are learning to test and experiment using this type of data. They are borrowing from the pioneering efforts of companies such as Amazon.com or Google, continuously using what's known as A/B testing not only to improve Web-site designs and experiences but also to raise real-world corporate performance. Many advanced marketing organizations are assembling data from real-time monitoring of blogs, news reports, and Tweets to detect subtle shifts in sentiment that can affect product and pricing strategy.

Advanced analytic software allows machines to identify patterns hidden in massive data flows or documents. This machine "intelligence" means that a wider range of knowledge tasks may be automated at a lower cost. As companies collect more data from operations, they may gain additional new revenue streams by selling sanitized information on spending patterns or physical activities to third parties ranging from economic forecasters to health-care companies.

Despite the widespread recognition of big data's potential, organizational and technological complexities, as well as the desire for perfection, often slow progress. Gaps between leaders and laggards are opening up as the former find new ways to test, learn, organize, and compete. Planning must extend beyond data strategy to encompass needed changes in organization and culture, the design of analytic and visualization tools frontline managers can use effectively, and the recruitment of scarce data scientists. Decisions about where corporate capabilities should reside, how external data will be merged with propriety information, and how to instill a culture of data-driven experimentation are becoming major leadership issues.

Social Technology

Social technologies are much more than a consumer phenomenon: they connect many organizations internally and increasingly reach outside their borders. The social matrix also extends beyond the joint creation of products and the organizational networks. Social Technology has become the environment in which more and more business is conducted. Many organizations rely on distributed problem solving, tapping the brainpower of customers and experts from within and outside the company for breakthrough thinking. Other research shows, how searching for information, reading and responding to e-mails, and collaborating with colleagues take up about 60 percent of typical knowledge workers' time—and how they could become up to 25 percent more productive through the use of social technologies.

Companies also are becoming flatter and with no borders, able to reach across units speedily and to assemble teams with specialized knowledge. Major organizations have invested in powerful social-technology platform that supports microblogging, content tagging, and the creation and maintenance of communities of practice. Benefits include accelerated knowledge sharing, shorter product-development cycles, and faster competitive response times. Companies still have ample running room, though for only a small percentage of the executives believe that their organizations will realize any substantial value from the use of social technologies to connect all stakeholders: customers, employees, and business partners.

Social features, meanwhile, can become part of any digital communication or transaction—embedded in products, markets, and business systems. Users can "like" things and may soon be able to register what they "want," facilitating new levels of commercial engagement. When social perceptions and user experiences influence product selection and satisfaction, the potential impact of social technologies on revenue streams can be enormous.

Automating knowledge

Physical labor and transactional tasks have been widely automated over the last three decades. Now advances in data analytics, low-cost computer power, machine learning, and interfaces that can understand humans are moving the automation frontier rapidly.

Developments in how machines process language and understand context are allowing computers to search for information and find patterns of meaning at superhuman speed. A Silicon Valley company that analyzes legal documents for pretrial discovery, machines recently scanned more than a half million documents and pinpointed the 0.5 percent of them that were relevant for an upcoming trial. What would have taken a large team of lawyers several weeks took only three days. Machines also are becoming adept at structuring basic content for reports, automatically generating marketing and financial materials by scanning documents and data.

At information-intensive companies, the culture and structure of the organization could change if machines start occupying positions along the knowledge-work value chain. Now is the time to begin planning for an era when the employee base might consist both of low-cost Watsons and of higher-priced workers with the judgment and technical skills to manage the new workforce. At the same time, business and government leaders will be jointly responsible for mitigating the destabilization caused by the displacement of workers and their reallocation to new roles. Retraining workers, redesigning education, and redefining the nature of work will all be important elements of this effort.

Think Intelligently and Survive - IBM's Watson and Cancer Research

Signaling a new milepost in the quest for artificial intelligence, IBM's Jeopardy-winning computer Watson has turned its attention to cancer research. Watson "trained" for the work by reading more than 600,000 medical-evidence reports, 1.5 million patient records, and 2.0 million pages of clinical-trial reports and medical-journal articles. Now it is the backbone of a decision-support application for oncologists at Memorial Sloan-Kettering Cancer Center, in New York.

Applying the Internet of All Things

Tiny sensors and actuators, proliferating at astounding rates, are expected to explode in number over the next decade, potentially linking over 50 billion physical entities as costs plummet and networks become more pervasive.

Through FedEx's SenseAware program, for example, customers place a small device the size of a mobile phone into packages. The device includes a global positioning system, as well as sensors to monitor temperature, light, humidity, barometric pressure, and more—critical to some biological products and sensitive electronics. The customer knows continuously not only where a product is but also whether ambient conditions have changed. These new data-rich renditions of radio-frequency-identification (RFID) tags have major implications for companies managing complex supply chains.

Companies are starting to use such technologies to run—not just monitor—complex operations, so that systems make autonomous decisions based on data the sensors report. Smart networks now use sensors to monitor vehicle flows and reprogram traffic signals accordingly or to confirm whether repairs have been made effectively in electric-power grids.

New technologies are now allowing people to become highly involved in their healthcare by using devices that monitor blood pressure and activity—even sleep patterns. Leading-edge ingestible sensors take this approach further, relaying information via smartphones to physicians, thereby providing new opportunities to manage health and disease.

Everything we sell now is a service that might have a hardware element in it

The buying and selling of services derived from physical products is a business-model shift that is gaining steam. An attraction for buyers is the opportunity to replace big blocks of capital investment with more flexible and granular operating expenditures. A prominent example of this shift is the embrace of cloud-based IT services. Cosmetics maker Revlon, for example, now operates more than 500 of its IT applications in a private cloud built and operated by its IT team. It saved $70 million over two years, and when an entire factory, including a data center in Venezuela, was destroyed by a fire, the company was able to shift operations to New Jersey in under two hours. Moves like this, which suggest that cloud-delivered IT can be reliable and resilient, create new possibilities for the provision of mission-critical IT through internal or external assets and suppliers.

This model is spreading beyond IT as a range of companies test ways to monetize underused assets by transforming them into services, benefitting corporate buyers that can sidestep owning them. Companies with trucking fleets, for instance, are creating new B2B businesses renting out idle vehicles by the day or the hour. And a growing number of companies with excess office space are finding that they can generate revenue by offering space for short-term uses. The Los Angeles Times has rented space to film crews, for example. Cloud-based online services are feeding the trend both by facilitating remote-work patterns that free up space and by connecting that space with organizations which need it.

Other companies are seizing opportunities in consumer markets. Online services now allow rentals of everything from designer clothing and handbags to college textbooks. Home Depot rents out products from household tools to trucks. IT that can track usage and bill for services is what makes these models possible.

Companies have much to discover about the efficiencies and flexibility possible through re-visioning their assets, whether that entails shifting from capital ownership to service use or assembling assets to play in this arena, as Amazon.com has done by offering server capacity to a range of businesses. Moreover, an understanding of what is most amenable to being delivered as a service is still evolving—as are the attitudes and appetites of buyers.

Engaging the new digital citizens

As incomes rise in developing nations, their citizens are becoming wired, connected to mobile computing devices, particularly smartphones that will only increase in power and versatility. Although several emerging markets have experienced double-digit growth in Internet adoption, enormous growth potential remains: India's digital penetration is only 10 percent, and China's is around 40 percent. Rising levels of connectivity will stimulate financial inclusion, local entrepreneurship, and enormous opportunities for business.

As Internet-enabled smartphones and other mobile devices move rapidly down the cost curve, they will enable vast new applications and sources of value. An accelerator of the value to come is the success of mobile-payment services across a number of developing economies. Dutch–Bangla Bank Limited (DBBL), in Bangladesh, for example, garnered over a million mobile-payment subscribers in ten months. Standard Bank of South Africa reduced its origination costs for new customers by 80 percent using mobile devices.

Another source of value is local matching services that connect supply with demand. Kenya's Google-backed iHub project uses technology services to identify and finance entrepreneurs. Technology also helps multinationals adapt products and business models to local conditions. In India, Unilever provides mobile devices to rural distributors, including traditional mom-and-pop stores. The devices relay information (such as stock levels and pricing) back to the company, so Unilever can improve its demand forecasts, inventory management, and marketing strategy—raising sales in rural stores by a third.

Digital meets physical experience

The borders of the digital and physical world have been blurring for many years as consumers learned to shop in virtual stores and to meet in virtual spaces. In those cases, the online world mirrors experiences of the physical world. Increasingly, we are witnessing an inversion as real-life activities, from shopping to factory work, become rich with digital information and as the mobile Internet and advances in natural user interfaces give the physical world digital characteristics.

Today's apps use smartphone technology to sense our locations and those of our friends or even allow us to point to foreign street signs for quick translations. Augmented reality will go further with next-generation wearable devices such as Google Glass, which deploys cameras and wireless connections to project information, on demand, through eyeglasses. Other wearable technologies are also gathering steam, from "intelligent textiles" to wristwatch computers that can not only display e-mails and texts but also run mobile apps. Technologies pioneered in game consoles allow us to use physical movements and gestures to interact with digital devices.

Companies are applying these technologies to experiences that have remained resolutely physical, creating a new domain of customer interaction. Food retailers Tesco have deployed life-size store displays at subway stations. The screens allow commuters waiting for trains to use smartphones to order groceries, which are then shipped to their homes or available for pickup at a physical store location. Other retailers are using similar displays in their physical stores so consumers can easily order out-of-stock products. Macy's has installed "magic mirrors" in store dressing rooms: a 72-inch display that allows shoppers to "try on" clothes virtually to help them make their selection.

Businesses are also integrating the digital world into physical work activities, thereby boosting their productivity and effectiveness. Boeing uses virtual-reality glasses so that factory workers assembling its 747 aircraft need to consult manuals less frequently. Annotated pop-ups point to drilling locations and display proper wire connections. Executives need to examine their businesses to find areas where immersive experiences or interactive touch points can stimulate engagement with customers. And they should reflect on the potential for interactive digital platforms to play roles in product design and marketing or in gathering customer feedback. These possibilities will grow in importance as customers and employees come to expect interaction between heightened digital and physical offerings.

Personalized and Simple

After two decades of shopping, reading, watching, seeking information, and interacting on the Internet, customers expect services to be free, personalized, and easy to use without instructions. This presents a challenge for business, since customers expect instant results, as well as superb and transparent customer service, for all interactions—from Web sites to stores.

A number of businesses have battled in the free-services arena against tough digital competitors. Users will probably never pay for many valuable technology-enabled services, such as search—and the list seems to be growing rapidly. Providers of these "free" services will need to innovate with alternative business models. The most successful are likely to be multisided ones, which tap large profit pools that can be generated from information gathered by an adjacent free activity that is commercially relevant. A familiar example is Google's policy of offering its search services free of charge while garnering revenues at the other side of the platform by selling advertising or insights into customer behavior. In a world of free, the hunt is on for such monetization ideas. More and more companies, for example, are exploring opportunities to sell to third parties or to create new services based on sanitized information that they have utilized completely.

Consumers expect to be treated as valued individuals. In the online world, Spotify and Netflix analyze their customers' histories to create "for me" experiences when recommending music and movies. Services are becoming even more hassle-free online: new Web and mobile apps are designed to be so easy to use that instructions are no longer needed. The demand for "immediate, quick and easy" is compelling companies to modify how they deliver real-world offerings—for example, by allowing customers to photograph checks and deposit them using smartphone apps, or buy authorizing transactions using their finger print scanned instantly on their mobile phone.

A world of digitized instant gratification and low switching costs could force many businesses to seek innovative business models that provide more products and services free of charge or at a lower cost. They will have to think about offering more personalization in their products and services and customization at a mass level. This approach could require changes to back-end systems, which are often designed for mass production. Businesses will need new ways to collect information that furthers personalization, to embed experimentation into product-development efforts, and to ensure that offerings are easy to use.

Mobile digital commerce

The rise of the mobile Internet and the evolution of core technologies that cut costs and vastly simplify the process of completing transactions online are reducing barriers to entry across a wide swath of economic activity. New technology platforms are enabling peer-to-peer commerce to replace activities traditionally carried out by companies and creating new kinds of payment systems and monetization models. Entry costs have fallen to the point where people who knit sweaters, for example, can tap into a global market of customers. Daimler Benz launched the car2go service, which rents out small electric cars by the minute in European, Canadian, and US cities. Amazon.com's Mechanical Turk and Task Rabbit host peer-to-peer marketplaces where independent contractors bid for tasks such as proofreading documents, pet sitting, or housecleaning.

Mobile-payment networks, sometimes augmented with services that extend beyond pure transactions, are a second area of evolution for e-commerce as costs fall. Starbucks envisions extending its pioneering use of smartphones for payments to include instant photo verification of buyers. New mobile-commerce platforms that manage transactions can offer customers the option of paying with credit credentials they established for other merchants.

This trend will become more striking over the next decade or so: 600 cities, most in emerging markets, will account for roughly two-thirds of the world's GDP growth. One likely consequence for fast-growing cities will be the rapid development of dense, digitally enabled commerce— new, highly evolved ecosystems combining devices, payment systems, digital and technology infrastructure, and logistics.

Transforming government services in health care and education

The private sector has a big stake in the successful transformation of government, health care, and education, which together account for a third of global GDP. They have lagged behind in productivity growth at least in part because they have been slow to adopt Web-based platforms, big-data analytics, and other technological innovations. Technology-enabled productivity growth could help reduce the cost burden while improving the quality of services and outcomes, as well as boosting long-term global-growth prospects.

Many governments are already using the Web to improve services and reduce waste. India has enrolled 380 million citizens in the world's largest biometric-identity program, and plans to use the system to make over $50 billion in cash transfers to poor citizens, saving $6 billion in fraudulent payments. In 2011, the US government introduced a Cloud First policy, which laid out a vision to shift a quarter of the $80 billion in annual federal spending to the cloud from in-house data centers, thus saving up to 30 percent on the cost of the shifted work. Governments can also use IT to better engage citizens, as South Korea has done with its e-People site, which helps citizens send online civil petitions for policy changes or reports of corruption.

Technology also is opening new opportunities to contain rising health-care costs and improve access. In rural Bangladesh, 90 percent of births occur outside hospitals. A mobile-notification system alerts clinics to dispatch nurse–midwife teams, who are now present in 89 percent of births. In China, a public–private partnership created a cardiovascular-monitoring system that allows patients to self-administer electrocardiograms and transmit data to specialists in Beijing, who can suggest treatments by phone. At New York's Mount Sinai Hospital, a venture with General Electric uses smart tags to track the flow of

CHAPTER 9

The New Intelligent World

We live in a very exciting technological era, in a continuously connected world were very soon we will be implanted with a chip that can monitor us and protect us by predicting our biology, our physiology, our needs and plan the necessary processes for us that will make our lives better. It can predict what meal we should have by the time we reach our home or restaurant because it analyzed our physiological requirements. It can order food for us after giving us options on our iPhone or Google glasses that we might wear, or displayed on the car's dashboard or on our iPad or laptop screen.

It will monitor our health and inform the medical staff of our required emergency attention. It can monitor our organs and inform the 3-D Printer that is linked to our stem cell generator to print a kidney and store it for one's kidney is failing. All this is possible if we are monitored and connected internally.

The Connectivity of Every Thing

We live in a very exciting technological era, in a continuously connected world where very soon we will be implanted with a chip that can monitor us and protect us by predicting our biology, our physiology, our needs, and plan the necessary processes for us that will make our lives better. It can predict what meal we should have by the time we reach our home or restaurant because it analyzed our physiological requirements. It can order food for us after giving us options on our iPhone or Google glasses that we might wear, or displayed on the car's dashboard or our iPad or laptop screen.

It will monitor our health and inform the medical staff of our required emergency attention. It can monitor our organs and inform the 3-D Printer that is linked to our stem cell generator to print a kidney and store it for one's kidney is failing. All this is possible if we are monitored and connected internally.

As objects and recently human, become embedded with sensors and gain the ability to communicate, the new information networks will create new business models, improve business processes, and reduce costs and risks. In most organizations and businesses, information travels along familiar networks. Business information is lodged in databases and analyzed in reports and then sent up the management chain. Information also originates externally—gathered from public sources, collected from the Internet, or purchased.

The physical world itself is becoming a type of information system. In a network of pathways called the Internet of Things, a term used recently by many thinkers, sensors and actuators embedded in physical objects—from roadways to pacemakers—are linked through wired and wireless networks, often using the same Internet Protocol (IP) that connects the Internet. These networks collect continuously huge volumes of data that flow to computers for analysis.

When such objects can both sense the environment and communicate, they become tools for understanding complexity and responding to it swiftly. What is revolutionary in all this is that these physical information systems are now beginning to be deployed, and some of them even work largely without human intervention. The best obvious example is the Mars probe that was blasted into orbit, and when it landed on Mars, it collected soil samples, analyzed them and sent the data to earth, millions of miles away.

For humans, minute micro-cameras already traverse the human digestive tract and send back thousands of images to pinpoint sources of illness. Precision farming equipment with wireless links to data collected from remote satellites and ground sensors can take into account crop conditions and adjust the way each part of a field is farmed. Billboards in Japan peer back at passersby, assessing how they fit consumer profiles, and instantly change displayed messages based on those assessments.

When a customer's buying preferences are sensed in real time at a specific location, dynamic pricing may increase the odds of a purchase. Manufacturing processes studded with a multitude of sensors can be controlled more precisely, raising efficiency. And when operating environments are monitored continuously for hazards or when objects can take corrective action to avoid damage, risks and costs diminish. We have cars that can park and drive themselves. We have cat food dispensers that can dispense food when the cat owner is away and many more from monitoring the insulin in your body to measuring your sleeping habits to improve your focus and rest.

Advances in wireless networking technology and the greater standardization of communications protocols make it possible to collect data from these sensors almost anywhere in the world at any time. Ever-smaller silicon chips for this purpose are gaining new capabilities, while costs are falling. Massive increases in storage and computing power, some of it available via cloud computing, make number crunching possible at very large scale and declining cost.

As these technologies mature, become smaller and more robust, the range of corporate deployments will increase. Now is the time for business leaders to structure their thoughts about the potential impact and opportunities likely to emerge from the Internet of Things.

Applications could be grouped into two categories: Information Collection and Analysis, and Implementation and Control.

Information Collection and Analysis

As the new networks link data from products, company assets, or the operating environment, they will generate better information and analysis, which can enhance decision making significantly.

When products are embedded with sensors, companies can track the movements of these products and even monitor interactions with them. Business models can be fine-tuned to take advantage of this behavioral data. Location sensors are already installed in customers' cars. That allows insurance companies to base the price of policies on how a car is driven as well as where it travels. Pricing can be customized to the actual risks of operating a vehicle rather than based on proxies such as a driver's age, gender, or place of residence.

Sensors and network connections are embedded in a rental car: it can be leased for a short time spans to registered members of a car service, rental centers become unnecessary, and each car's use can be optimized for higher revenues. Zipcar has pioneered this model, and more established car rental companies are starting to follow. In retailing, sensors that note shoppers' profile data (stored in their membership cards) can help close purchases by providing additional information or offering discounts at the point of sale. Market leaders such as Tesco are at the forefront of these uses.

In the business-to-business marketplace, one well-known application of the Internet of Things involves using sensors to track RFID (radio-frequency identification) tags placed on products moving through supply chains, thus improving inventory management while reducing working capital and logistics costs.

The range of possible uses for tracking is expanding. In the aviation industry, sensor technologies are spurring new business models. Manufacturers of jet engines retain ownership of their products while charging airlines for the amount of thrust used. Airplane manufacturers are building airframes with networked sensors that send continuous data on product wear and tear to their computers, allowing for proactive maintenance and reducing unplanned downtime.

Data from large numbers of sensors, deployed in infrastructure or to report on environmental conditions, can give decision makers a heightened awareness of real-time events, particularly when the sensors are used with advanced display or visualization technologies.

Security personnel, for instance, can use sensor networks that combine video, audio, and vibration detectors to spot unauthorized individuals who enter restricted areas. Some advanced security systems already use elements of these technologies, but more far-reaching applications are in the works as sensors become smaller and more powerful, and software systems more adept at analyzing and displaying captured information.

Logistics managers for airlines and trucking lines already are tapping some early capabilities to get up-to-the-second knowledge of weather conditions, traffic patterns, and vehicle locations. In another application, law-enforcement officers can get instantaneous data from sonic sensors that can pinpoint the location of gunfire by analyzing the recorder sounds of gun shots.

The Internet of Things also can support longer-range, more complex human planning and decision making. In the oil and gas industry, the next phase of exploration and development could rely on extensive sensor networks placed in the earth's crust to produce more accurate readings of the location, structure, and dimensions of potential fields than current data-driven methods allow. The payoff: lower development costs and improved oil flows.

In retailing, some companies are studying ways to gather and process data from thousands of shoppers as they journey through stores. Sensor readings and videos note how long they linger at individual displays and record what they ultimately buy.

In health care, sensors and data links offer possibilities for monitoring a patient's behavior and symptoms in real time and at relatively low cost, allowing physicians to better diagnose disease and prescribe tailored treatment regimens. Patients with chronic illnesses, for example, have been fitted with sensors in a small number of health care trials currently under way, so that their conditions can be monitored continuously as they go about their daily activities.

Implementation and Control

Using collected live data the basis for automation and control means converting the data and analysis collected through the Internet of Things into instructions that feedback through the network to automated controllers that in turn modify processes. Closing the loop from data to automated applications can raise productivity, as systems that adjust automatically to complex situations make many human interventions unnecessary.

The Internet of Things is opening new frontiers for improving processes. Some industries, such as chemical production, are installing legions of sensors to bring much greater granularity to monitoring. These sensors feed data to computers, which in turn analyze them and then send signals to actuators that adjust processes—for example, by modifying ingredient mixtures, temperatures, or pressures. Sensors and actuators can also be used to change the position of a physical object as it moves down an assembly line, ensuring that it arrives at machine tools in an optimum position. This improved instrumentation multiplied hundreds of times during an entire process, allows for major reductions in waste, energy costs, and human intervention.

In the pulp and paper industry, for example, the need for frequent manual temperature adjustments in lime kilns limits productivity gains. One company raised production 5 percent by using embedded temperature sensors whose data is used to automatically adjust a kiln flame's shape and intensity. Reducing temperature variance to near zero improved product quality and eliminated the need for frequent operator intervention.

Networked sensors and automated feedback mechanisms can change usage patterns for scarce resources, including energy and water, often by enabling more dynamic pricing. Utilities such as Enel in Italy and Pacific Gas and Electric (PG&E) in the United States, for example, are deploying "smart" meters that provide residential and industrial customers with visual displays showing energy usage and the real-time costs of providing it. Based on time-of-use pricing and better information residential consumers could shut down air conditioners or delay running dishwashers during peak times. Commercial customers can shift energy-intensive processes and production away from high-priced periods of peak energy demand to low-priced off-peak hours.

The most demanding use of the Internet of Things involves the rapid, real-time sensing of unpredictable conditions and instantaneous responses guided by automated systems. This kind of machine decision making mimics human reactions, though at vastly enhanced performance levels. The automobile industry, for instance, is stepping up the development of systems that can detect imminent collisions and take evasive action. Certain basic applications, such as automatic braking systems, are available in high-end autos. The potential accident reduction savings flowing from wider deployment could surpass $100 billion annually. Some companies and research organizations are experimenting with a form of automotive autopilot for networked vehicles driven in coordinated patterns at highway speeds.

Scientists in other industries are testing groups of robots that maintain facilities or clean up toxic waste, and systems under study in the defense sector would coordinate the movements of groups of unmanned aircraft. While such autonomous systems will be challenging to develop and perfect, they promise major gains in safety, risk, and costs. These experiments could also spur fresh thinking about how to tackle tasks in inhospitable physical environments that are difficult or dangerous for humans.

What's next?

The Internet of Things has great promise, yet business, policy, and technical challenges must be tackled before these systems can be widely embraced. Industry groups and government regulators should study rules on data privacy and data security, particularly for uses that touch on sensitive consumer information.

Liability frameworks, legal and moral, for the bad decisions of automated systems will have to be established by governments, companies, and risk analysts, in consort with insurers. Networking technologies and the standards that support them must evolve to the point where data can flow freely among sensors, computers, and controllers. Software to aggregate and analyze data, as well as graphic display techniques, must improve to the point where vast volumes of data can be absorbed by human decision makers or synthesized to guide automated systems more appropriately.

Within companies, big changes in information patterns will have implications for organizational structures, as well as for the way decisions are made, operations are managed, and processes are conceived. Companies can begin taking steps now to position themselves for these changes by using the new technologies to optimize business processes in which traditional approaches have not brought satisfactory returns.